Praise for Mike Errico

Mike Errico is an exemplary role model for lifelong learning and carrying teaching beyond the studio. His classroom blurs the binary between student and teacher, encouraging the voices of all students.—**Nominating committee, New York University's David Payne-Carter Award for Excellence in Teaching, 2019**

Mike Errico changed my life. He has an unwavering belief in his students' ability to succeed in whatever they set their minds to. This belief and support, along with his holistic approach to songwriting and dedication to helping students find their voice, made it possible for me to take leaps of faith that otherwise felt impossible.—**Hana Elion, Overcoats**

Mike Errico: for years, a songwriter's songwriter; challenging yet beloved educator at some of the nation's top universities; fantastic and respected musician; all-around witty, brainy, and fascinating conversationalist. I speak for myself, the entire professional music community, and the hundreds of students he has mentored when I say that Mike has not only great talent as a singer-songwriter, but is a gifted teacher and storyteller, with unique and valuable insights into songwriting and the creative process. I have learned so much about music—and everything—from him.—**Bob Power, producer/mixer (D'Angelo, Erykah Badu, the Roots, A Tribe Called Quest); arts professor, Clive Davis Institute of Recorded Music, New York University**

As a guest in Mike Errico's classroom, I've witnessed a true expert in his craft at work. His insight into songwriting is something that only a seasoned composer and musician can really know and one that his students eagerly ingest, knowing that their own craft is already improving through Mike's unique life's-lessons-learned experience.—**Pete Ganbarg, president of A&R, Atlantic Records**

Mike Errico is able to match passion and experience—to connect the dots for his students and offer the insight and guidance that helps them convert thought into expression. The power of song matters, deeply, to Mike, and that faith, along with boundless curiosity, lights up a classroom—or a stage.—**Alan Light, music journalist; author; SiriusXM radio host**

I've been a fan and friend of Mike's for years. He's an artist's artist—independent, boundary pushing, and deeply interested in the creative process. He's fun and cerebral. He takes a real joy in cultivating the work of others, and has a way of building community around his work that I truly admire. And when I refer to "his work," I mean the many facets of Mike's wide talent: songwriting, performance, teaching, and writing.—**Brian Reed, host and cocreator of *S-Town*; senior producer of *This American Life***

While I was in school at the Clive Davis Institute at NYU, Mike was a sweet and supportive ear. He believed in my vision as a writer and artist, and always kept me on target to reach and exceed those dreams.—**Madison Emiko Love, singer-songwriter (Selena Gomez, Katy Perry, Lady Gaga, Camila Cabello, Ava Max)**

Mike has been a dear friend, collaborator, and advisor for years, so I've seen him excel in numerous capacities across the music and entertainment industries. I can't think of anyone more capable and passionate about instructing the next generation of songwriters and music visionaries. His book will be a generous gift to students everywhere.—**Vivek J. Tiwary, author of** *The Fifth Beatle*; **CEO, Tiwary Entertainment Group (***Jagged Little Pill, American Idiot, The Producers***)**

Mike is the most caring teacher and human; he goes above and beyond for his students, being sure to teach not only about art, but what it means to be an artist. He is always available to meet you for a cup of coffee, and will be a source of comfort and rationality if you cry in public at said meeting.—**Khaya Cohen, producer; songwriter; singer, Moon Kissed**

It's a maniacal time to be a young musician, and Mike's a peerless guide. He's sharp-eyed, big-hearted, road-tested, and—most important—supremely curious about the past and future of popular music. His class gave me a map for creative living.—**Hans Bilger, songwriter; multi-instrumentalist**

I wish I'd had a teacher (and a class) in school like Mike's. He invests so much in the students . . . the vibe is so nurturing and supportive. When I came in as a guest speaker, even though every student had their own individual projects, it felt like I was talking to a team. There was that kind of unity, in a really cool way.—**Matt Nathanson, recording artist**

Mike Errico teaches songwriting with a mastery of narrative and empathy and humor that makes his courses unforgettable experiences for our students.—**Dan Charnas, author; associate arts professor, Clive Davis Institute of Recorded Music, New York University**

As a colleague of Mike Errico, I've had the pleasure to work with him and to watch him share his creative talents with no reserve or expected return on his tireless investment. So, it's no surprise that he would also selflessly share them with the rest of the world. With a raw and uncut human approach to songwriting, production, and discipline, I can attest that you will find no one more genuine, experienced, and real to learn from.—**Joanne "Josie" Carrero, electronic producer; artist and founder, Pretty Hybrid Records; adjunct professor, Clive Davis Institute of Recorded Music, New York University**

Mike Errico is a creator who understands the deep connections between forms—music, writing, and more. I always look forward to hearing what he has to say.—**Jacob Slichter, author; drummer, Semisonic**

Mike's deep-thinking, left angle/right angle approach to analysis is always inspiring. He's able to tie together seemingly disparate observations in a holistic way that resonates with students and fellow teaching colleagues alike.—**Brian Long, artist manager; vice president, Knitting Factory Management; adjunct professor, Clive Davis Institute of Recorded Music, New York University**

I've been lucky to be connected to Mike in many ways over the years—as writer, artist, and educator. He approaches all parts of his musical journey with the same level of enthusiasm, curiosity, and energy, and his expertise and impact are clear. His insights into songwriting, particularly with the lens of the current business and creative conditions, are extremely valuable.—**Molly Neuman, global head of business development, Songtrust**

Mike Errico is an incredible teacher and mentor with an intuitive sense for how to help students become the best versions of themselves. He approaches creative development from every angle you can imagine, and just about any student would benefit from his wisdom and experience. I'm very grateful to have studied under him at a pivotal moment in my songwriting trajectory.—**Sarah Solovay, songwriter (Jason Derulo, Icona Pop, Aloe Blacc, Steve Aoki)**

He's soulful, smart, and very funny. One minute you'll be howling over one of his slow groove story songs. Then he'll punch you in the emotional gut with a quiet gem—a perfect distillation of life, love, loss. He's a killer singer, monster musician, masterful storyteller, and teacher. There's no pigeonhole for him. Just listen up. Because you're going to want to go wherever it is he's taking you.—**Jonatha Brooke, recording artist**

Mike's ability to identify, clarify, and synthesize abstract ideas makes him hugely valuable in the classroom, and rare among artists. He has a wellspring of cultural knowledge, a curiosity about ideas matched only by his creativity in expressing them, and a generosity of spirit evident in everything he does. —**Jessica Helfand, designer; educator; author; founding editor,** ***Design Observer***

Mike is not only a veteran of music, education, and musical education; he is an advocate for the interesting. His approach to teaching and art making encourages artists to lean into the unconventional, abandon the industry "conveyor belt," and create a colorful, interdisciplinary career that serves artists and entrepreneurs of all fields. Mike reminds us that to make art, one does not need to "suffer," nor even just survive—an artistic life can and should be fruitful, fulfilling, and fundamentally freeing.—**Molly Kirschenbaum, songwriter; multimedia artist**

Mike is a brilliant singer-songwriter and teacher. But Mike is also a poet and a social critic whose songs range from the deeply emotionally evocative (there are some I can't listen to without crying) to funny, edgy, sardonic, profound, filled with wisdom. Mike is wise about the world, about relationships and serendipity, about both the mundane and the sublime. His was the music I kept coming back to when I was writing my first novel. Mike Errico's lyrics and his voice became the soundtrack to that novel and actually helped me to realize the full extent of the emotion I needed to translate into my characters. Mike is a gift for both his fans and for the students who are lucky enough to study with him. He makes us all better writers.—**Juliann Garey, author,** *Too Bright to Hear Too Loud to See* **(winner, American Library Award for Best Fiction)**

Mike's approach to music is equal parts masterful and reckless. Each note and lyric is vetted through the lens of his experience as a road-savvy touring artist, and delivered in a manner afforded only to those with a true and nuanced command of the art form. Working with Mike has, on a professional level, been uniquely gratifying.—**Jamie Siegel, producer; mixer (Lauryn Hill, Sting, Patrick Stump, TV on the Radio, Joss Stone)**

Mike Errico is a unique combination—a fantastic artist/songwriter who also happens to be an incredible teacher. On top of that, he brings a powerful academic perspective. It is rare that a single individual can easily move between all of these worlds, and Mike is one of the few who can both create art and compellingly explain the processes by which it is made.—**Dan Freeman, music producer; bassist; music technologist, Clive Davis Institute of Recorded Music, New York University, and the Juilliard School**

As a songwriting professor, Mike Errico shares his extensive knowledge of the songwriting process with the next generation of songwriters, producers, and artists. Anyone aspiring to get into songwriting or the music industry would benefit tremendously from Mike's knowledge and expertise.—**Timothy Pattison, director of creative at BMI**

Mike is full of interesting perspectives, insight, and opinions on the state of today's music industry, as well as the ins and outs of songwriting and composing. I love the coffees, beers, and discussions we have had over the years with all his funny anecdotes and stories from real-life experiences on the road, in the studio, and in the classroom.—**Stein Bjelland, Chair of Music Norway, appointed by the Norwegian Ministry of Culture**

Mike Errico is a brilliant songwriter who has been immersed in the NYC music scene for years. His experience as an artist who has released several independent recordings required him to become an expert of the inner workings of the music industry. As a result, he has become one of the most popular teachers at NYU's Clive Davis Institute of Recorded Music. His practical and thoughtful approach to teaching and sharing advice from his own personal career pursuits make him a standout in the music business education field.—**Linda Lorence-Critelli, president of the New York Chapter, the Recording Academy; former vice president of Writer Publisher Relations, SESAC; assistant professor, Rider University**

In universities, there are often two types of teachers: those who pursue grants and accolades at their students' expense, and good teachers. Mike Errico is the third type of teacher. He speaks about songwriting as a human being, not just an industry expert. Students left his class not only informed, but transformed, and enlivened with the same passion and curiosity that first compelled them to pick up a guitar or keyboard and try to write a song.—**Ben Lapidus, singer-songwriter; playwright**

Mike Errico brings a lifetime of songwriting knowledge in a universal language everyone desires. I've taught alongside him at NYU and he's a pro's pro. Nothing but respect and love for Mike when he leads a classroom.—**Joe D'Ambrosio, founder, Joe D'Ambrosio Management**

Mike Errico is that rare thing: He's an original. Soulful, funny, and searing. And he's also a gem of a person. Which is a happy bonus.—**Jonathan Bernstein, artistic director, the Performing Arts Project**

If I were looking for songwriting advice, I'd call Mike Errico. His wise, intuitive insight into the art of the song is steeped in hardcore experience and presented with humor and compassion. . . . He loves songwriting. And he loves teaching songwriting. But more importantly, he's soulfully genuine in the way he shares it all with us.—**Machan Taylor, songwriter; educator; singer (Pink Floyd, Sting, Gov't Mule, Aretha Franklin)**

Mike Errico is a master songwriter with a cult following like no other. He teaches as all masters do: with grace, good humor, and inspiring generosity of spirit.—**Dr. Kevin Hicks, president, Stevenson School**

MUSIC, LYRICS, AND LIFE

MUSIC, LYRICS, AND LIFE

A FIELD GUIDE FOR THE ADVANCING SONGWRITER

MIKE ERRICO

Backbeat
Books

Guilford, Connecticut

Backbeat Books
An imprint of Globe Pequot, the trade division of
The Rowman & Littlefield Publishing Group, Inc.
4501 Forbes Blvd., Ste. 200
Lanham, MD 20706
www.rowman.com

Distributed by NATIONAL BOOK NETWORK

British Library Cataloguing in Publication Information available

Library of Congress Cataloging-in-Publication Data

Names: Errico, Mike, author.
Title: Music, lyrics, and life : a field guide for the advancing songwriter
 / Mike Errico.
Description: Lanham : Backbeat Books, 2021. | Includes bibliographical
 references and index. | Summary: "Music, Lyrics, and Life is the
 songwriting class you always wish you'd taken, taught by the professor
 you always wish you'd had"— Provided by publisher.
Identifiers: LCCN 2021022240 (print) | LCCN 2021022241 (ebook) |
 ISBN 9781493059874 (cloth) | ISBN 9781493059799 (epub)
Subjects: LCSH: Popular music—Writing and publishing.
Classification: LCC MT67 .E77 2021 (print) | LCC MT67 (ebook) | DDC
 782.42/13—dc23
LC record available at https://lccn.loc.gov/2021022240
LC ebook record available at https://lccn.loc.gov/2021022241

Knowledgeable, available, kind, and honest.
Sometimes gets distracted by tangents.

—Anonymous, end-of-semester student evaluation

CONTENTS

INTRODUCTION

Hi, I'm Your Songwriting Professor

I was born backward. Literally. It's called a "frank breech birth," which is doctor-talk for "ass-first." The joke is that I never quite turned around, and there's some evidence to support that.

I backed into songwriting. My dad, a classical pianist, signed up for a pop songwriting class at New York's Songwriters Hall of Fame. He hated it but didn't want to ask for his money back. We have the same name, so I showed up in his place. I've gone on to record deals, international tours, and music for TV and film.

I backed into teaching. While on the road, I got a call from a friend, a college dean, who invited me to speak to students about songwriting as a career. I told him I didn't think I knew how to do that. He booked me anyway. I've been teaching ever since.

And I backed into this book. The one I wanted to give my students didn't exist, so I wrote it.

My point: People come to songwriting from all different directions. Some have wanted to do this since they were little kids. Some like to make their parents mad. Some are wildly talented but crippled with doubt. All I can say is that no matter which way you're facing, I think I can help you.

I say this because I've been teaching college-level songwriting for years now, and every semester I have students who want to meet with me for office hours. This means they *volunteer* to sit with me—no credit, no cash payout, just coffee—and some of them aren't even in school anymore. The ones who are often take my classes multiple times. My inbox is packed with demos, remixes, and private links to upcoming releases. They're all repeat customers, and over the years, I've noticed that many of them ask repeat questions. The point of this book is to try to address those repeat questions because chances are good that you have them, too, and I can't have coffee with everyone, much as I'd like to.

I've gone into this book knowing what's already available for songwriters on bookshelves and on the internet. For example, if you want to know where a chorus should land in your song, there's an *actual* chorus of YouTubers dying to tell you to make it happen early. Online schools and master classes at any price point are available to separate you from your time and money. You can go on a two-week songwriting retreat at a French chateau featuring all-inclusive wine-and-cheese tastings. I assume some of these options are valid, or at least fun. But this book is different because it's not about doling out songwriting answers—it's about figuring out what you're even asking, and then helping *you* find answers that work best for you.

We'll get into some technical aspects of songwriting, but let's also recognize the context in which we're writing because one has a huge influence on the other. As we speak, genres are cross-pollinating, songs are getting shorter (except for the ones that are getting *much* longer), the history of recorded music is in your pocket, and no one knows what that music is worth or how to compensate its creators. The concept of *stereo*—music for your left ear and your right—is under siege by future formats. New surround-sound recording gear is being brought into university studios, and no one's completely sure what it'll be used for. Death itself is in retreat—as of this writing, deceased pop stars are going on tour as holograms.

Meanwhile, some of my most talented former students are taking their music-making skills and going to work at artificial intelligence platforms—they're creating playlists and full compositions that change with the arc of the sun, your astrological sign, or the collective algorithm of you and whoever's in the hot tub with you.

Accelerated transition creates anxiety, and over thousands of cups of coffee, I've seen that anxiety play a huge role in what students think they're even *able* to write. Collectively, we idle in a low-key tech-induced panic mode at all times. We watch our machines approach sentience while we ourselves lollygag at the speed of human evolution: historically speaking, we've just started wearing pants, for crying out loud. And it is not helpful that our product—*music*—is invisible. The satisfaction we receive is not as tactile or primal as it might be if we were to make, say, a baby, a chair, or a pizza.

Meanwhile, dangerous myths about "the life" continue to swirl around this profession. They're vicariously thrilling—antiheroic, fast-and-wild pop star fantasies lived for our viewing pleasure—but the fact is, every semester I've taught, a major international artist has either taken their life or died in some way that is directly traceable back to "the life." Looking at my students now and wondering who I'd pick for that kind of success, my answer is "Not. A. Single. One." I think the cure (or at least a treatment) requires unpacking the entire vocation.

- What is success?
- What is a hit?
- What is a song?
- Why am I doing this?

And ultimately,

- Who am I, and how can I live with whoever that reveals itself to be?

These are all songwriting questions, and if your songs aren't asking them of *you*, chances are good they aren't asking them of your *listeners*. Without them, I don't know what kind of songs you'd be writing—cultural propaganda, I guess. Anthems for Late Capitalism. And you know? There's a lot of money in that. Can you guess why? Because every flag needs to fill the solemn, awkward silence as it crawls up the pole. One of the main questions this book will ask you is, *Which flag are you writing for?* I'll also ask you to plant one of your own.

Anti-Market Marketing

Right off the bat, I have a strong recommendation: don't chase the market. If you were to do that with food, the data-driven fact would be that McDonald's is the best restaurant in the world. They sure have sold a lot of Big Macs. But if you saw me bearing down on one, I doubt you'd say, "Yeah. That Mike. Gotta hand it to him. He knows quality."

This is my bias, but I don't think your long-term goal is to make more Big Macs. Thelonious Monk wrote, "A genius is the one most like himself." Here's a shocker: *being the one most like yourself is hot*.

This idea is not new, and somehow it's always new, and if you suddenly feel like you're walking in the dark, then you're in the right room. Finding your voice and being able to deliver it—that's the revolution. And that's what I hope I can help you with.

Let's Get to Work

At the beginning of every semester, I hand out Sister Corita Kent's "Ten Rules for Students and Teachers." John Cage popularized it by posting a tweaked version on choreographer (and life partner) Merce Cunningham's studio wall.

TEN RULES FOR STUDENTS AND TEACHERS

RULE 1: Find a place you trust, and then try trusting it for a while.

RULE 2: (general duties as a student)

Pull everything out of your teacher.

Pull everything out of your fellow students.

RULE 3: (general duties as a teacher)

Pull everything out of your students.

RULE 4: Consider everything an experiment.

RULE 5: Be self-disciplined. This means finding someone wise or smart and choosing to follow them. To be disciplined is to follow in a good way. To be self-disciplined is to follow in a better way.

RULE 6: Nothing is a mistake. There's no win and no fail, there's only make.

RULE 7: The only rule is work. If you work, it will lead to something. It is the people who do all the work all the time who eventually catch on to things.

RULE 8: Don't try to create and analyze at the same time. They're different processes.

RULE 9: Be happy whenever you can manage it. Enjoy yourself. It is lighter than you think.

RULE 10: We are breaking all the rules, even our own rules, and how do we do that? By leaving plenty of room for "x" qualities. (Added by John Cage)

Helpful Hints:

Always be around.

Come or go to everything.

Always go to classes.

Read everything you can get your hands on.

Look at movies carefully and often.

SAVE EVERYTHING. It might come in handy later.

I hand it out because it sets a tone of bravery and eliminates the risk associated with it. I want—I *need*—spectacular experiments from you, and in return, I want to help you build a controlled environment. In music, you don't get a lot of those.

Four Big Ideas

When I teach, I touch on four main themes and weave them through pretty much everything. In the back of the book, I recommend outside materials that go deep on each.

Big Idea One: Journaling

Journaling is the unrestricted generation of raw material from which work can be made. It's probably the most important Big Idea of the bunch because it's the most flexible, and the most willing to stray into the heart of whoever's doing the generating. Please do it and pay attention to whatever comes out, because if your journal morphs into an artist's sketch pad or a schematic for a circuit board, you should follow that trail. Follow it right out the window. The songwriting rainbow ends where all rainbows end—in mist. Which is where they originate. So take your ticket out and enjoy where it leads.

Big Idea Two: Mechanics

What's *happening* in the songs you love, or the popular songs on the charts, and what can we use in our own work? I liken this to an owner's manual you should actually read. Why? Consider buying a lawnmower, tossing its manual, assembling it incorrectly, and then firing it up—blades and pistons showering your lawn, hot metal grazing your neighbor's labradoodle. The blackened patch on your lawn. The ire. The lawsuits.

Might you actually luck out and hack together a bitching robot and be hailed a genius? You might. You might even go viral with your lawnmower-robot, which would be cool. But, from my experience, the former scenario—dead labradoodle—is the more likely. Even bitching robots adhere to laws of mechanics, and it's really useful to know what they are.

To that end, we'll get granular, logical, and clear. There will be graphs, and lists, and troubleshooting items.

Big Idea Three: The Wisdom of Your Fellow Practitioners

These are the people who've internalized the mechanics, blown up a few lawnmowers, and are willing to share what they've learned. They are generous mentors, and that makes them indispensable.

Big Idea Four: Constantly Asking, "Why?"

What binds the mechanics to the practitioner and the practitioner to the page? As poet Mary Ruefle put it, "Why did you come here, to this place, if not in the hope of being understood?"

These are big questions, and in search of answers, professors compile monstrous packets full of barely interconnected interviews, essays, star maps, and rants that students download or pick up at the campus copy shop. They are accidental things of beauty, these packets. I love the mismatched fonts and cockeyed scans; I appreciate the hastily drawn-in brackets and triple exclamation points that stress key ideas. I've collected packets from other professors, and flipping through them feels like what it must be like to ski off-trail in high powder, free of tourist traffic and warning signs. They are unrestrained, exhilarating searches for answers to the question, "Why?"

The Upshot

While it's true that several of my past students have gone on to enormous success, a lot of my students aren't going to end up being songwriters at all. I don't count either as personal success or failure. Can you imagine if your high school physics teacher based their worth on how many of their students became famous physicists? The asylums would be full of high school physics teachers. And yet, so many principles that were learned in physics are applicable to other fields and to the living of a richer, more informed life.

This means you don't have to be a lifelong career songwriter to benefit from this book, and I wrote it that way on purpose. My students don't need to write another song in order to lead successful lives using material we covered. If you study anything deeply, everything eventually seems to meet up.

That said, here's my hope for you: I want you to have a tight, incandescent song that will kick the door down for all your visions to rush through. I want you to plant a flag so that you can build a creative world around it, and I want that world to be intrinsic to who you are as an artist. I want you to crash your own set lists with a wave of brilliant new songs, and I want you to play them out in public places where you'll make money, fans, lovers. And I want you to make this world a more beautiful place.

I wrote this book the same way I write songs—I started with a question, followed it, and hung on for the ride. I'd like to thank my students for asking great questions and to thank you for showing up. If you've gotten this far, the book's already a hit; if you get to the end, it's a smash; and if you're writing better songs, it's a movement.

Mike Errico
Brooklyn, NY
February 15, 2021

One

TERMS OF SERVICE

We can't talk about how to do something without agreeing on what it is we're trying to do. So, let's get some terms straight.

What Is a Song?

We're working within the framework known as *pop music*. We all have a general notion of what that is, but to clarify: Please don't throw your guitar down the staircase and tell me you've written a new "song" because the artist in me will agree. The only problem is that I can't inform or advise you on that impulse—so let's call that kind of thing "out of bounds."

If you're disappointed, well, so am I. Could we talk about whether the staircase should've been carpeted? Or whether this collision of iconographies forms a sonic metaphor of the twenty-first century? Oh, sure. Could we title your opus something snappy like "Soundtrack to *Nude Descending a Staircase*"? Absolutely. Coffee was invented for ridiculous conversations, and I'm available by appointment. But let's agree that it falls outside the scope of this conversation. Sorry.

Instead, here are two goalposts. They're arbitrary, sure, but if you think about it, the North Star isn't really "north," either, and we've still managed to navigate by it.

Left goalpost: A "song" is a piece of music that uses established song forms both from history and from the present-day pop charts.

Our songs may be new, but there's an older story at work within them. Song forms are not hard, the way an oven is not hard to operate. It's the "getting something edible to come out of it" that's the trick.

Right goalpost: There's a definition of art that writer George Saunders gives in his essay "Mr. Vonnegut in Sumatra."

> I began to understand art as a kind of black box the reader enters. He enters in one state of mind and exits in another. The writer gets no points just because what's inside the box bears some linear resemblance to "real life"—he can put whatever he wants in there. What's important is that something *undeniable* and *nontrivial* happens to the reader between entry and exit.

That's it. Deliberately and satisfyingly vague. *Did it move you?* If the answer is "yes," then the form you used to make it happen is immaterial.

Every song we write will be in some relation to these goalposts. The mission, then, is to decide where in the balance between them we want a song to land. When we're *really* lucky, we don't get to decide—the song does. Some songs want to use traditional forms the way water fills a bucket. Others break the forms into the shapes they need to finish themselves. In those moments, it's not entirely clear who's doing the writing, who's in the room, who's pushing the pen or finishing the melodic phrases without your conscious assistance. These are magical moments that keep songwriters coming back over and over, and that sense of runaway songwriting never fully leaves the finished product. You can hear it in there, forever.

Goalposts? *Really?*

If you're like some of my students, you're already annoyed, and the fact that there are rules makes you seethe. Here are some favorite comments:

"How does anything ever innovate that way?"

"Are you just telling us to copy forms that already exist? How is that creative?"

"How are *you* creative?"

I get it. Form is boring and reductive, and, by association, so am I. So let's look at the pop charts. (This is *pop* music, after all, and "pop" is short for "popular.") If we charted out the top five songs, chances are nearly 100 percent that traditional song forms will be sitting there, simple and agonizing on the page. (We'll talk about what those forms are, soon.) There are slight variations and a few clever moves, but each is beholden to some underlying agreement about what works.

Music isn't original in this regard, by the way; it's not like painters have it any different. I mean, pick a painter, throw a dart: 99.99 percent of their canvases are squares or rectangles. Does that enrage you? Do you spit on the floor of the Louvre and say, "One more artist's vision, suffocated by the shape of the canvas!" My guess is it doesn't even come up. Reason: The vision transcends the frame.

And it's not just an "art thing," either. Outside Detroit, near the airport on I-94, there's a giant tire—and I mean, like, eighty feet high—that at one point had a huge nail jammed into it. It was an ad for a puncture-resistant tire from Uniroyal, and one time when I drove past it, I started thinking about how new tires get invented. What were their research-and-development (R&D) meetings like, after years spent puncturing a zillion tires and reporting the results? Engineers in white lab coats probably said things like, "Well, we used this kind of rubber, and such-and-such steel belts, wrapped in such a way, and the dang thing popped on us anyway, so we tried X rubber, but this time we . . ." and on and on.

Was anyone like, "You know . . . maybe the problem with the tire . . . *is the shape of the tire.* Maybe the fact that it's a circle is what's holding us back from our dream of puncture-proofness. Maybe we should look at, say, triangle tires? Something rhomboid? Trapezoidal? Whattya say, team?"

My point: That never happened. Why? Because circular tires work. Circles are good. They aren't sitting there at Uniroyal labs, trying to *reinvent* the wheel. Why? Because *round rolls*.

Wait . . . What Do *You* Know about Tire R&D?

Nothing . . . but! A few years after I saw that giant punctured Uniroyal, I met Jennifer Basl, a mechanical engineer *who designs tires for Goodyear*. How could I not ask her my "tire shape" question?

> *So, what is your job, exactly—you design tires?*

> My specific role is designing the tread pattern and what we call the cavity shape.

> *And they don't have that down yet?*

> [*Laughs*] It's just a tire, right? It's round, it's made of rubber—you know, how hard could it be? But once you get into the finer details, it gets a lot more complicated. There are a dozen or more other performance characteristics that we're considering. And it's always about finding the right balance between all of those things for a particular application because unfortunately there is no such thing as a perfect tire, yet. Otherwise, we would have made it.

> *My contention is that, when you're at an R&D meeting, no one comes up with the idea that the tire shape is the variable that will make puncture-proofness a reality.*

That is correct. As far as I know, in Goodyear's 120-year history, we have never made a tire that wasn't round, and we've had a lot of really smart people working for us. It's just never been a viable option.

What would you say are the major problems with a square tire?

[*Sighs audibly*] Where to begin? If a tire has to do one thing well, that one thing is roll, right? And squares don't roll.

And what would a perfect tire look like?

Well, it would be round, to start with . . . I mean, the laws of physics have to be obeyed, and the tire has to be round within that framework. We have all sorts of options for what we can do—the compounders and chemists have dozens of different combinations of raw materials, and I have nearly infinite options designing the tread pattern and the profile shape. So, it's all just about finding the right combination of things that work—within that overarching constraint of keeping it round.

Is there anything radical on the design horizon?

We're always coming up with new concepts and out-of-the-box prototypes, like a 360-degree spherical tire that we don't have a direct consumer application for—I don't think there's an actual vehicle that we could test it on. It's all just simulated at this point.

So, that would be a moment where the "roundness" of a tire is actually being challenged by a forward-thinking concept . . .

Uh . . . it's still round. It's even *more* round. It's round in all directions. So you just can't get away from the roundness, no matter how much you want to.

What About Right Angles?

Earlier, I mentioned spitting on the floor of the Louvre over visual artists' penchant for right-angled canvases. Instead of guessing why that is, I asked John Currin, the internationally celebrated painter whose work has moved from Willem de Kooning–styled abstraction to Renaissance-influenced satires of old Danish porn. Consistent through it all: Canvases enclosed in right angles.

Part of an artist's job is to engage with the constraints of their medium. How do you approach the constraints of yours?

To me the most compelling thing about painting is that you've seen it a million times, but it's always a kind of miracle that it's a flat thing—there's no "inside" of the painting. It's an exalted space, and what never ceases to delight and amaze me is how simply pushing a little bit against the flatness of the painting makes that space appear. Figures feel alive and have emotions, but it's a frozen dream, you know? It doesn't exist. The building block of that is the spatial illusion, and I guess within the pop song there are certain forms that are just as useful.

There definitely is a shared language . . .

I like things written and done in a style that's shared. I like genre painting and genre music. For the same reason, I would do goofy-looking paintings of women—you know, kind of porny stuff—because I found that within the genre, I could connect in my peripheral vision, metaphorically speaking, with the *real* thing that I'm maybe suppressing or that I just can't see unless I'm looking through this genre. So both on a personal level and on a stylistic level, it opens me up to those constraints.

Speaking of constraints: Most of your work is contained within right angles. Does that ever bother you?

Oh no, no, not at all. I mean, partly it's just the two dimensions. And the upper corners have a certain special kind of real estate. The lower corners are also very important—different things happen in the corners than in the center of the canvas. Even when I was making abstract paintings, I always had a feeling about the lower left corner. A lot of my favorite paintings have this. There's a Venus in the National Gallery in London by Bronzino [*Venus, Cupid, Folly and Time*, circa 1545] that has this beautiful dove just fitted into the lower left corner. And that famous painting by Titian [*The Bacchanal of the Andrians*, 1523–1526]—it's a whole bunch of people dancing around, and there's a nude woman fitted into the lower right corner. But no, I don't feel oppressed by the rectangle at all. I don't much like *squares*, I will say that.

That was my next question . . .

I've never really been able to make a painting on a square. I find squares to be ugly. I can do paintings *off*-square, like if one side is 1 and the other side is 1.1. I mean, I guess squares are okay on the *ground*, you know, like a square courtyard or a square room. I'm not an architect, I don't know whether square rooms are good or not, but square windows are ugly. There's something about them I just don't like.

Has adhering to the common language of right angles become a necessity over time? Do other canvas shapes just call too much attention to themselves?

Well, I think I see what you're getting at; it's that formal radicalism sends you into a cul-de-sac. But I think it's also just natural. It's like a common tone or interval in music or your mother calling you—some birds will use the same intervals, and it's just a thing that goes through nature. I think there are many aspects of that in all art forms that people either consciously or unconsciously are using just to make people feel like they're in the world and that they're home.

Where did that start? Is it as simple as its ease of construction?

Well, you know, if you're not in a cave and you want to make a post and a lintel, you're making a rectangle. If you want to make parallelograms, they'll fall on your head, you know? And then there's gravity. I mean, one of the things that was cool about the movie *Alien* (2001) was the idea that, in space, things aren't load bearing, so you have these stretched hexagonal doors, and it's not about resisting gravity and spanning a gap, you know? You're not supporting weight. But if you live on a *planet*, you kind of need rectangles.

It seems like part of being "modern" or "futuristic" is about building spaces that break away from right angles.

I think that's a problem. What is it, [Frank Gehry's] Bilbao or whatever—it's like *you can't hang paintings*, and you realize that paintings sort of do, I guess, depend on the architecture. You know, the whole point of a painting is to give a sort of relief from the reality of the wall. Right? It's a hole in the wall and a reprieve from the real, but it has to echo the wall, I guess. Certain symmetry is extremely important in terms of your body or the way you feel. Like, you want your bed to be level. If you've ever slept on an un-level bed, it's not a good feeling. You start to realize that the *intentional* rejection of a lot of these standards creates a lot of problems.

So, we can say that the fact that you operate within right angles has not hindered your career.

[*Laughs*] No!

Conclusion

Form is our *ally*, and whatever we do creatively will be in some relation to it. It's the same for Steven Spielberg, Versace, Lady Gaga, and flying squirrels who probably wish they were actually flying but are really just dropping out of the sky, albeit elegantly.

So, What's a *Good* Song?

For us, at this stage, there really is no usable answer to that question because it's not about creation; it's about judgment. Judging is easier than doing, which is why everyone has an opinion, but not everyone has a song. So, forget it.

Instead of judging, we can discuss why a song resonates in a given moment, we can situate it somewhere in our personal histories, and we can signify a ritual it enhances, but in the end, a core mystery remains unsolved. There's a life force within a song that resists capture; calling it "good" is one of our failed attempts.

So, let's not troll ourselves by judging what we, at heart, don't even understand and call a "good" song something simple and localized, like one that speaks *to you* and that tells *your* story the way *you* want it to be told.

What Is a "Hit" Song?

Is Leonard Cohen's "Hallelujah" a "hit" song? Well, you'd probably call it one *now*, but it barely registered upon its release. What changed? Not the song.

That's significant because you're writing the song, not its trajectory.

Obviously, there are songs that are listened to more than others. This is a business as much as an art, and anyway, we'd like for people to actually hear what we're expressing. So, here are two potential definitions of a "hit song," with a recommendation to follow:

> **Industry definition:** A hit is a song that the greatest number of people have heard via radio, streaming, TV, and so on.

Easy enough. It's the song at the top of whatever chart you're paying attention to. You've got a song? They've got a chart. And they're itching to judge whether it's a hit—by this definition.

A lot of writers want to write toward the charts, and there are songwriting classes geared specifically for them. To me, what would be great is if you could take a course like that the year *before* a particular type of "hit" is released because if you're writing "hits" based on what's presently on the charts, you've already missed that boat. The people who wrote that present-day "hit" have already written the follow-up, the follow-up to the follow-up, the chill house remix of the follow-up to the follow-up—you get the point. A "hit" to the industry is in the rearview mirror of the people who wrote it.

> **Workable writer definition:** A hit is a song that satisfies the circle of people who love your work and also widens that circle to some extent.

Here's what I mean. Let's say you write a song, and your mom loves it, but your dad hates it. Okay, fine. You have a fan base of one. So, you write another song, and your mom loves it, again ("You're so talented!"), but now your dad has come around, too; Mom even catches him whistling the hook around the house. You now have a percentage fan increase of 100 percent. You've doubled your fan base! Good on you. A song that increases your fan base two, five, or ten times is a "hit" regardless what your actual numbers are or whether the charts ever find out about it. That's a ratio increase that anyone *on any level* would love.

Is this optimistic? Yes. I am unapologetically optimistic for you. Optimism is armor. Pick it up, put it on, and shield yourself from the onslaught of useless distraction.

A Recommendation: Output

Chasing that first definition (a "hit" is the one at the top of the charts) will drive you insane because that's not something you can control. Hits are a function of all kinds of outside forces: who's dating who, who messed up on social media, who killed it at an award show, who's got an amazing marketing team, who *died* (sorry, but it's true), who got incredibly lucky. That's not to take away from anyone's talent, but that *is* to say that whatever you write walks into a world of chaos called, well, the world.

What *can* you control? Your *output*. The *amount* of writing you do. The people on the charts are also people who write *a lot*—every day, all kinds of music, whether you know about it or ever hear the songs or not. It's a constant process, and *that part of the songwriter's life is squarely in your hands*. Concentrate on that, and all other definitions become, if not predictable, then at least possible. "Quantity begets quality," says every book on writing, but I'll add: Quantity begets quantity, and quality begets slap fights over what "quality" even means.

Quantity also means *finishing*. Finish doesn't mean "fall in love with." But until it's finished, it can't be a hit, or good, or an album track, or—anything. Once it's finished, it can be *anything*.

Let's Review

1. A song is a conversation between you and history. Song forms are snippets of a conversation that began long before you got here.
2. A "good" song is a conversation between you and yourself; a "hit" song is a conversation between you and your fans; everything else is just traffic.
3. Not all "good" songs are "hits." Not all "hit" songs are "good." A song can't be either until it's finished.

Two

SOME TOOLS

Whether or not we've ever written a song in our lives, we have collected some powerful tools for songwriting. Let's rummage through our tool kit and marvel at their functionality. We have the following:

An Opinion

When you ask someone what kind of music they listen to, do they ever say, "Oh, you know. Everything"? Well, that's a lie. *Nobody* listens to everything, and most people listen to very little. In *Hit Makers*, Derek Thompson reports that 90 percent of the music we listen to *is stuff we've already heard before and want to hear again*. That leaves ten percent of total new listening to cover the history of recorded music and maybe—*maybe*—a few of the bazillion new pop releases that come out on a daily basis. What do I mean by a "bazillion?" As of spring 2021, nearly 60,000 songs were uploaded to the Spotify streaming platform—*per day*. How many do you think you've checked out?

I get that we all want to appear open-minded, and we're probably not actively *avoiding* a lot of music (for the most part), but we're absolutely not listening to "everything." What if, instead of being ashamed of that, we champion our opinions—and admit them?

Assignment

Here's a little homework—it's *life*work, really. As you read this book, make a playlist for yourself of around fifteen songs that you absolutely love. These are songs you wish you wrote; songs you can't live without; songs that take you back to a place in time; songs that feel like they open a door to somewhere you can't fully explain. *Songs you aspire to.*

Be honest. Be shameless. Keep the playlist to yourself. Stare daggers at anyone who uses the term "guilty pleasure." Pleasure is pleasure. Guilt is somebody else's problem being dumped on you. "Javert's Suicide" from *Les Misérables* is a fine choice. "Bananaphone" by Raffi, great. Only Taylor Swift songs, sure. Write it down. Make a playlist. *Admit it.*

Why would you do this? Because these choices shape your musical taste, and they contain clues to what will satisfy you in your own writing. There are chord changes, and timbres, and arrangements, and lyrics that are already leaking into whatever you've been writing; this playlist is you, finding the origins of the leak.

Target Practice

Now picture being included *on* this playlist, alongside the songs that have inspired you. What would it take? By creating a target (which is what this playlist is), you can point your creative energy in a worthy direction. Why would you do this? Consider taking archery class without using a target. Where would you aim? Does letting an arrow fly make you an archer? Or are you just a hazard to those around you?

If you're an established writer or a seasoned pro looking to take your writing down a different lane, try making a playlist that reflects your ambitions. Treat it like an aspirational mood board, but dissect it, investigate it—draw lines of commonality between your choices. Those common threads are all jumping-off points for a new aesthetic for you.

Each Other

Jane Wagner, who wrote comedian Lily Tomlin's stage show *The Search for Signs of Intelligent Life in the Universe*, observed that "reality is nothing but a collective hunch." In music, the collective is, basically, whoever you're able to collect and have a hunch with. This is why songs are road-tested, audience-tested, radio-tested; mixes are run by friends, family, producers, sullen teens; vocals are mixed up, and down, and up in some places and down in others.

When you're in a collective, you fabricate the hunch that is later referred to as "reality." By admitting who/what you are via your playlist, you'll be that much closer to finding who you want to be collectively hunching with.

Which brings up another point: as a part of a collective, each member helps maintain that reality. Together, you set a tone. So, be good to each other, and be good to yourself. Not only is kindness a better place to live, but whatever you put out will come back to you, whether you ever know it or not.

Three

GOD? Y/N

I dated a freelance puppeteer for a couple of months. She had a friend who dressed like a pirate (black-and-white striped shirts, scraggly beard, tricornered black hat, functionless eye patch). The pirate drove a jewel-encrusted Ford Econoline with the chassis of a VW Bug welded on top and decorated to look like an actual giant bug. He filled a metal box in the back of the van with dry ice and made money freezing rubber bugs into ice cubes and selling them out the side door. One night, we hatched a plan to sell enough frozen bugs to finance a trip to Burning Man. One-way. (In case you're wondering: No, the numbers don't work.)

Long story short, I never did make it to Burning Man—the puppeteer left with the pirate, and I was left with a handful of rubber roaches, new respect for Jim Henson, and a forgotten copy of *The Artist's Way* by Julia Cameron.

This is an example of "synchronicity," which is something like coincidence, but so "on the nose" that it seems planned by unseen forces. All I know is that I needed to read this book, and in its extravagant delivery, it showed me how much.

In case you don't know it, *The Artist's Way* is a staple in artistic circles. It's sold millions of copies internationally, spawned workshops and seminars, and remains an invaluable tool for creative people in every medium. It's the self-help *Star Wars*, and I'd never heard of it, but from the moment I brushed the rubber bugs off the cover and turned to "Week One," I was hooked.

In *The Artist's Way*, Cameron lays out a twelve-week process of "creative recovery" that basically mirrors the twelve-step program of Alcoholics Anonymous. She explains that within us is an "artist child" who is boundless but also impetuous, jealous, and moody. Over the course of our lives, this child may have been wounded (bad circumstances, others' expectations, bottled anger, regret, and so on), and in order for us to counter the damage, we must create the conditions that will allow this child to thrive. Cameron challenges readers to address their spiritual damage and to make the sometimes-terrifying life changes necessary to recover—or uncover—their artistic selves.

I assign *The Artist's Way* in some of my classes, hoping my students will see similar benefits. Some do, but others have offered a contrasting perspective that goes to the heart of a creative practice. They point to another way. Maybe you'll relate.

Students have told me they don't buy the woo-woo brand of self-actualization that hippie-types have accessorized with crystals, drum circles, and white-people fire walks; they see a brand of spirituality that can be the province of some really weak thinking and some terrible art. They've also grown up sensitized to the abuse of borrowed philosophies, particularly from the East, and particularly by the West. I've been told that the label "recovering artist" is presumptuous. Some students just feel that "stuff happens," and it's good, or it's bad, but that doesn't warrant "recovery"; it's just called "life." They note that there's as much profit to be made in telling people they're "special" as there is in telling them they're "wounded" and "recovering." They're not subtle, my students, and I love them for it.

But it's when the "God Concept" comes up that things really go off the rails. Cameron states that recovery requires "engaging the Great Creator," and she asks the reader to be open-minded about surrendering to a higher power: "Goddess, Mind, Universe. . . . The

point is not what you name it. The point is that you try using it."
My ex–altar boy Catholic self was cool with that, but to others, the
idea that an external spiritual force is needed to empower oneself
creatively means accepting a submissive role that they see as coming
from an oppressive tradition. *Who came up with this "higher power"*
dynamic, anyway? And who wrote the texts? And who controls the
language with which the texts were written? Welcome to one more
manifestation of a broken, biased system, with me beholden to it in
order to access my own creativity.

This kind of feedback keeps me up at night. Arguing for or against
a higher power is not my goal—my goal is to answer a more immediate question: Can we be productive in the presence *or* absence of a
God Concept? And, if so, can we get back to work without dropping
books like *The Artist's Way* in a fire? I believe so.

Fact: We're all going to die. Few agree on what happens next—
Heaven, Hell, the Bardo, Paradise, Hades, the spirit world, round-
trips back as someone/something else. A less celebrated option is
that when we're dead, we're just dead. Finished. There is no soul and
no other plane for the dead to travel to or the living to dialogue with.
The body reabsorbs into the earth, and life goes on. The End.

For students who have a higher-power problem, I focus on that
last option.

What does death provide if we decide there's nothing on the other
side of it? Well, urgency, for one. By acknowledging its finality, we
place our hopes, aspirations, and energy on *this* side of the grave.
Death asks, *How are we spending our increasingly valuable time?*
If you take the question seriously, it's hard not to strive to become
more accountable to the present moment. And that's another thing
death provides: presence.

What does this have to do with songwriting? Everything. Because
if there's an afterlife, then death is stripped of its meaning, and, if
we're not careful, we are relieved of the need to value our precious,

irretrievable time. And what do we do when we don't value our time? We waste it.

See, *that's* where I get annoyed.

And I'm not alone, because both the divine and the secular worlds agree: time wasters suck.

> "So it is: We are not given a short life but we make it short, and we are not ill-supplied but wasteful of it. . . . Life is long if you know how to use it."—Seneca

> "To be idle is a short road to death and to be diligent is a way of life; foolish people are idle, wise people are diligent."—Buddha

> "A man who wastes one hour of time has not discovered the value of life."—Charles Darwin

> "O Allah, I seek refuge in you from incapability and laziness." —Islamic Du'a

> "Go to the ant, O sluggard, Observe her ways and be wise, Which, having no chief, Officer or ruler, Prepares her food in the sum-mer And gathers her provision in the harvest."—Proverbs 6:6–8

Both the divine and the secular worlds are united in the dislike of time wasting, and both approaches can even coexist. In Martin Luther King Jr.'s last speech, he laid them side by side, saying, "It's all right to talk about the new Jerusalem, but one day, God's preacher must talk about the new New York, the new Atlanta, the new Phila-delphia, the new Los Angeles, the new Memphis, Tennessee." Higher ground and common ground don't cancel each other out. In this instance, they are part of a balanced picture.

This is why, when I see someone slacking in class, I'm stunned. I want to tell them, "Why are you here, if you're not invested? Run! Run like your hair's on fire! Get to where you need to be! God or the Existential Void—whichever one you ascribe to—is coming! Your actions tell me that you either don't know this or you don't believe it. But that is untenable! *There is no third option!*"

Why am I going on about the value of death? It's because I've read my student evaluations. Well, I don't actually read them—my wife does while I curl into a ball in the corner. But she tells me that, consistently, the thing students like the most about my class is—get this—*deadlines*. And I can't help but think they're aptly named— deadlines!—because, in their small way, deadlines provide urgency and give meaning to time. And what do we want if not meaning and purpose?

So, if you like deadlines, here's one for you: death. There's your final deadline.

And if you see death as a portal to an afterlife, here's a deadline for you: the Day of Judgment, when your work will be appraised, and you'll find out where you'll be spending eternity.

Which one do I ascribe to? Who cares! It's your obituary you're writing, every single day. Are you too tired? Did you need to binge- watch something?

Your priorities are always showing. Strung together, they paint a larger portrait—a work of art called *Who You Are*.

Four

YOUR NEW ATTENDANCE POLICY

I've been told that a great way to keep students on their toes is to give pop quizzes. To make sure students are on time, I should have the pop quiz be the first thing we do in class. The questions should be about the reading. The results should count toward their final grade.

On one level, fine, I get it. But mostly, I don't. Yes, pop quizzes might make you work, but they don't make you *want* to work. Timing them at the beginning of class might make you show up, but they don't guarantee your *presence*. And sure, they'll affect the final grade, but eventually that grade will manifest as the weird abstraction it always was. (What is a B+, *really*?) Meanwhile, the muscle of self-discipline that might have grown by nurturing sustainable habits will yield to the sag and flap of atrophy. Fact: A gym hasn't been invented where the bench does your bench presses for you.

A Fork in the Road

1. If you don't want to be a songwriter, don't. Honestly, it's too hard to be "kind of" into it. I could say the same about starting a business, getting married, or making illegal fireworks—all these things require more passion than a pop quiz will ever inspire.

2. If you're "on the fence," consider the fence; someone who was only "kind of" into fence making may have built it. Low commitment does not make for a sturdy fence. Suggestion: Get off

the fence. One way or the other. Be a songwriter—or don't. "Death by fence"—not what you want on your toe tag.

3. Recognize that you're here. You're reading this. That's a clue.

If you *do* want to do this . . .

"Your Presence Is Requested"

Jesus said, "Many are called, but few are chosen," and *I'm not correcting Jesus*, I'm just clarifying a step that's implied: Even fewer of those who are called can *handle* having been called. Several will try to justify letting The Call go to voice mail—"I'm not ready." "I'm not good enough." "Maybe it's spam." "Maybe *I'm* spam."

That's all standard, stock-issue resistance, and when people say, "Half the game is just showing up," I think this is what they're talking about. Either (1) destiny calls and the call is answered, or (2) destiny calls . . . and waits . . . and decides not to leave a message.

Being a no-show is one thing, but what about showing up late? I mean, you *did* show up, so does that count as *half* of "half the game"? No, it does not.

We have a moral responsibility to each other. We also have a moral responsibility to each other's time. Why? Because we don't get that much of it. Embedded in assignments, meetings, song forms, lengths of albums, shows, and sentences is an implicit deal between both parties: don't waste my time, and I won't waste yours.

Lateness breaks that deal. It's a breach of contract. And it's not just an opinion of one's own time—it's a value judgment on someone else's. It's like a Participation Tax: *Dealing with me means dealing with having to wait for me*, which means it's an insult, ultimately. And if that insult becomes a pattern, it gets baked into your reputation. Reputations don't un-bake easily, and people who value their limited time will eventually protect it from you—by not meeting with you. Doors will close.

Lateness is a crime that steals from whoever commits it.

Here Comes a List

Instead of giving you a pop quiz, I'll just say: If you're writing furiously, hounding people for feedback, and fashioning a *lifestyle* that allows you to show *yourself* what you're capable of, you'll have done yourself one of the greatest favors of your career—and your life.

Here's a policy that is unwritten and un-policed yet somehow strictly enforced. And to make it sound official, let's call it "Attendance Policy for Musicians."

This is what it looks like.

1. If you're late, you're off the gig.
2. If you're not the second coming of John Lennon and John Coltrane combined and you're late, you're off the gig.
3. If you *are* the second coming(s) of those two, then you're on the gig until you slip, or tastes change, or you get lazy (or lazier). Then? You're off the gig.
4. If you were going to deliver a track or a song to a publisher or music house for placement with a client or artist or brand or anything, but you were late? You're off the gig.
5. If you're late for the gig, know that music people—cowriters, bandleaders, booking agents, publishers, frontpeople, managers, composers, producers, rhythm sections, wedding bands, inconvenienced brides—will talk, because it's a small, small world, and everybody knows everybody. You will then get a rep, and you'll be considered unreliable, and you'll be off gigs *you didn't even know you might have had.* By not getting that call? You're off the gig.

6. If you're not the second coming of Mozart and Maria Callas, no one will *care* that you're off the gig. No one, that is, but you. Why will no one care? Because:

7. The line of people hoping for that gig extends beyond the limit of human sight.

The difference between that happening and not happening is this:

Be. On. Time. For. The. Gig.

What Does All This Mean?

It means that "attendance" is being taken from now on, and the "pop quiz" is every second of every day. We don't know how much time we have left, but we do know that, in the end, we'll have either done what we'd hoped to do, or not. Life is musical chairs; the song just stops.

People who understand this deserve to work with people who also understand this.

Five

BEHOLD! THE AWESOME POWER OF THE DAILY JOURNAL

Writing is a muscle, and journaling is going to the gym.

That's why the most important book I assign is full of blank pages: a journal. Every single writer I've had in as guest speaker journals in one form or another. Some of you may have been journaling since the days of diaries with the lock that didn't work and the key you lost anyway. That's a head start. But if not, I've taken cues from a few books to get you rolling.

Write Three Pages a Day, Rain or Shine, in Sickness and in Health, till Death Do You Part

In *The Artist's Way*, Julia Cameron refers to these as "morning pages." Let me see if I can anticipate your questions.

"Do they need to be done in the morning?" They don't.

"Are we expected to journal on holidays?" As if holidays exist. Give me a day on the calendar—any day—and I can find a holiday/reason not to write, work, get off the couch, or live. Maybe how often you journal is however much you care.

"What dimensions should the page be?" Three pages is three pages, and you *know* what three pages is. The page is not a postage stamp, and it's not the menu at Denny's. If that's not helpful, I'd say you can default to 8.5 by 11 inches, which is the standard size a copier will spit at you.

"Can I draw pictures?" Yes. Pictures, pressed leaves, band stickers, mugshots, whatever. It's your portable playground, and no one tells you what game to play. I do think it helps to start each entry with the date and a couple of quick surrounding details so that if you have to come back to a particular thought, a few sense memories might help you access your state of mind.

"Why *three* pages?" Because I think everyone's got a page and half in them, and it's mostly garbage. *It's hot outside. I have a head cold. Work sucks. It's laundry day.* Whatever. Once you've cleared that nonsense out, you've got a page and a half to go, and that's when things take off. You *have* to fill the space, so you do. What happens to me is that the writing starts to get ahead of the thinking, and the subconscious takes the wheel. That's exactly who should be driving, and it's why morning is good—you're still in a kind of suspended state between waking and sleep. People have tried to manufacture that in-between state, by the way. Salvador Dalí used to sit in a chair with a key in his hand and a plate on the floor; he'd relax until he started nodding off, and the key would drop and hit the plate. He'd wake up just a little woozy and liminal, which helped him continue to be Salvador Dalí. Whatever you have to do. But hit something and do it consistently, like, oh, reps at the gym.

Alternative: Pick a Specific Object and Write About It for Ten Minutes

Time yourself, and when ten minutes ends, stop, no matter where you've landed. This style of "object writing" is in *Writing Better Lyrics* by Pat Pattison, and it's a little more customized to time-sensitive, "on demand" styles of writing. Singer-songwriter Madison Cunningham came to class and told us she uses a loose version of this method and never misses a day.

> **"Why ten minutes?"** By focusing on an object and then diving fast and deep, you train yourself to get to the heart of an idea quickly. This is helpful when you're in cowriting sessions and you're thrown into a room with someone, maybe a total stranger (who's also famous), and given a specific prompt. Timing yourself trains you to brainstorm efficiently. It's like running wind sprints at—yes—the gym.

Journal, You Say? Where Might I Find One?

Selling journals looks like it's a pretty good business. There are a lot of choices. Some are scented. Some have no lines, like nightmares. Some have ribbon bookmarks, which is hilarious for a journal because *you know you left off where the words end, don't you?* There are even "songwriter's journals," which remind me a little of people who order lobster and are given bibs—kind of infantilizing. But I guess if you're selling blank books, you need to add value, and I respect the hustle.

I get my journal at the pharmacy in the aisle that still sells blank CDs, and I go alone because I will not be rushed, distracted, or spoken to. College ruled, obviously, with a metal spiral—plastic is just ridiculous. It speaks of a fragile life.

It has to be three-subject. One-subject notebooks are flimsy and too short; thoughts physically straddle the volumes, making it difficult to refer back to scribble that suddenly strikes me as genius. Color is critical! I let the color tell me which one I want to take home. This can take a while.

The point is, it's a ritual, and whether it's kicking one's cleats three times before stepping into the batter's box or heaving innocents into a volcano, we humans love ritual.

While You're There: Pens

Same aisle. Bold yet sensitive. Minimal drag but not excessively fast so that it slips out from under your grasp. I used to think the rubber grips were just for show, but I've grown to like them. They provide a sense of luxury. They say, *I'm worth it.* I assume people who go for weekend bike rides dressed like they're in the Tour de France can relate. It's a psychological edge. So go ahead. Treat yourself to the rubber grips.

Why Pens? Because of Longhand

I have a rule for journaling in my classes: it must be done longhand. No laptops, no in-app note taking. My students, so politically sensitive to one another, think nothing of attributing this rule to my age. To them, I suddenly appear decrepit, Gandalf-ian (minus the magic). They audibly groan that longhand is from another time— one of trees pressed into thin sheaves the Elders call "paper," to which a fancy quill is applied. Do they picture me at home, listening to their demos through an old-timey ear horn? Probably.

So. Let me explain.

Nature

I'm reminded that working on computers is *natural* at this point. "We are native users," I'm told, with the ageism implied. My thought is that we are more native to *ourselves* than we are to tech. Until the Singularity arrives (assuming it hasn't), that remains true. We are looking for clues to ourselves, and longhand leaves more distinctive footprints.

Efficiency

I'm aware that typing is efficient—I have a laptop, myself, and oh yeah, *I typed this book*. But here's a simple question: What is the point of being efficient at making something when we're not sure what we're making? "Efficiency" will be our friend—later on. For now, we're wandering around the mind in search of the raw thing we will apply the blade of efficiency to.

Convenience

Yes, typing is a convenient way of writing, but Hot Pockets are a convenient way of eating. You might love Hot Pockets, and that's fine, but you have to admit there's something about their unwavering uniformity that is psychically unsettling. I think of this when I type on a laptop and an A is an A is an A. That makes no sense! They're all different A's, all being used differently—the stresses and meanings are flattened by the recording mechanism. So much of the language of songwriting is in the performance, but computers specialize in Hot Pocketing whatever gets typed in. I mean, how do you account for the *performance* of the language on the computer? YOU CAN'T ALL CAPS EVERYTHING.

Nietzsche put it succinctly: "Our writing tools are working on our thoughts." To me, typing does it by erasing character—right at the moment when character is *exactly* what we're looking for. This isn't tech's fault; it just wasn't built to convey the specifics of who we are. It was created to convey the common denominators between us in order to serve as many of us as possible. Helvetica is speech in someone else's voice, and it works great—later on in the process, like on the lyric sheet or the recording contract. At the journaling phase, technology is a weak link in a game of telephone we play with the page.

When A Does Not Equal A

I think what intrigues us about cover songs is that we get to witness different artists' choices when faced with the same notes. Each variation argues that fixed writing has an endless number of shades and that a song can be recognizable and unknowable at the same time. The difference is performance. I'm reminded of the time a friend and I went to an exhibit at the Brooklyn Museum titled "Hip-Hop Nation: Roots, Rhymes, and Rage." After staring at empty tracksuits and Kangol hats for a while, one of us realized that, without Jam Master Jay walking in them, we were just staring at a pair of Adidas. We now refer to the exhibit as "Fat Laces in Glass Cases," and it's come to represent any moment when a detail can't stand in for the whole—when it's all sneaker, no swagger; all machine, no ghost.

Glorious Mess

Journaling is a nonlinear, visual art form with music in it that we can see. It speaks in our private voice. It reveals our character. Yes, there is writing in the *way* we write.

We may need graphic capability, moments for caricature, long division, exclamation points that gouge the page—who knows. Connecting lines are instructive; cross-outs are documents of where we've been. This is investigative action painting; like Jackson Pollock, we are recording the physical act of recording before assembling it in the medium of our choice. It's still a jumble, several needles in a haystack, with your longhand humming the internal music of whatever may emerge. On a laptop, that music comes out like quantized MIDI notes.

That's what fonts are, aren't they? They're quantized letters, sitting on a grid at mechanized distances. No swing. An A is an A is an A.

The slop and stink and ketchup stains and taped-in ticket stubs are the natural ecosystem that belches up song fragments. The performative aspects of your longhand have literal manifestation—they come out in tempo, arranging, choice of instrument, and personal opinion. Your journal records a live, first take of something it took a lifetime to process.

Physical Pain

Yes, I'm aware that your journaling hand hurts after a while. From what I'm told, *everything* hurts after a while. If you're looking to avoid pain, *every* business is the wrong business to be in.

"A Desirable Difficulty"

In 2014, Pam A. Mueller and Daniel M. Oppenheimer published a study in which they tested students' ability to absorb information while taking class notes in longhand versus on a laptop. They found, conclusively, that "students who took notes on laptops performed worse on conceptual questions than students who took notes longhand." They noted longhand's slower speed but its greater focus and synthesis—there was more *interaction* with the material. They noted that the longhand students wrote fewer words, and what makes sense is that a slower technique creates a need for word *choice*—a cognitive process that requires an understanding of the concepts. To me, that sounds a lot like a first edit taking place. Longhand was deemed "a desirable difficulty," whereas computer use generated more words but seemed to kick the cognition can down the road.

Surveillance

If you think these are grandpa reasons to journal in longhand, here's a more high-tech one: It's because they're eavesdropping. Who are "they"? I don't know, but they're staring at you through your camera and grabbing the keywords you're typing. They're serving you ads based on your emerging subconscious thoughts. *They're reading your journal.* Are you freaked out by that? And by "that" I mean "robots selling your unaccountable Franken-secrets back to you?"

I always took the Bob Dylan line "If my thought-dreams could be seen / They'd probably put my head in a guillotine" as a warning. If you're journaling on a laptop, *your thought-dreams can be seen.* What do "they" do with them? I don't know, but I mean, look at Mark Zuckerberg's face. He loses your data the way dogs lose tennis balls under the couch. He winds up in court and in front of congressional panels—a *lot.* The obvious takeaway: Your secrets aren't secret when you're typing them. Takeaway 2: You're not alone when you're alone at the computer. Takeaway 3: Your computer is not a tool you can trust. And you *have to trust your tools.*

You'd think this would be a golden age of longhand.

Maybe it is.

Where to Write

In *On Writing*, Stephen King says, "All you need is a door you're willing to shut." I'd add coffee to the list, but that's it. Annie Dillard is more brutal: "You can read in the space of a coffin, and you can write in the space of a tool shed meant for mowers and spades. . . . Appealing workplaces are to be avoided. One wants a room with no view, so imagination can meet memory in the dark." So goth. So good.

Priorities

Journaling requires you to make some time for it. If you like to get trashed and be up all hours but also find that your best writing happens early in the morning with a clear head, you're going to have to commit to one of those two jealous lovers. In presenting irreconcilable choices like these to my students, I have seen (some of) them change their habits. Some realize that being a better singer requires quitting smoking. Some realize far more profound changes than that, and the decisions push them toward prioritizing the creation of raw material, which is the root of the song, which is the root of everything.

Where to Look

We have tools, definitions, and pens . . . what now? Where do song ideas come from? The artists I've interviewed usually answer that question with a shrug. "It just came to me." "It was like I dictated it." "I sat bolt upright in bed and ran to the guitar." In other words, they don't know.

Nobody knows.

In *Catching the Big Fish*, film director David Lynch writes that the subconscious is like a river, ideas are fish, and desire is the bait. I really like that image, but just because you know where the fish are doesn't mean you know how to catch them. Luckily, I know a guy who does.

Greg Felt is the cofounder of ArkAnglers, a full-service fly-fishing business on Colorado's Arkansas River, where he's been a guide since 1985. In 2016, he was elected commissioner of Chaffee County; in 2020, Governor Jared Polis appointed him to the Colorado Water Conservation Board, where he represents the Arkansas River Basin—28,000 square miles and nearly a million people.

You basically work inside a giant metaphor.

Oh, yeah. You don't have to say, "Get ready for a metaphor." When you're talking about the river, you sort of weave in and out of it all the time. And I will say the river that I work on is a free-flowing, wild river—we fish it from about 10,000 feet in elevation down to about 5,000 feet, through all kinds of geology and geography. Some rivers are more formulaic.

What do you notice about people as they interact with the river?

One thing that's been interesting is that there's a lot of what some would call "superstition" involved. I always go back to Stevie Wonder: "When you believe in things that you don't understand," from that song, "Superstition." Working in a fly shop on a Saturday, you might have twenty or thirty people come in, and if it's a good day, they all have a theory as to what was going on or what was working. And when things aren't going well, all kinds of superstition starts to come in, and it becomes really clear they don't know what's going on. They have ideas that they try to match to very scant evidence. It's interesting how important it is for people to feel like they know what's going on, even when they don't.

What "scant evidence" are they working with?

What you have initially is the surface of the river. Sometimes you can see into it better and sometimes it's harder, depending on how clear the water is, how much reflection, or glare—all that. But you also have what you believe to be true about the river, and the fish, and the bugs. And for a lot of people, that's it. They just go to the river with their beliefs, and they throw their beliefs out there and see if they stick.

We try to coach people that there's a lot more information available, if you open up your mind a little more. I tell people, "Five minutes of observation is worth an hour of implementation." What does the river look like? What does the sky look like? What kind of day are we having? What's the wind doing? Are there clouds? Are the clouds coming? Are the clouds leaving? What are the birds doing? Some of these birds are focused on the same aquatic insects as the fish, and if you spend enough time out there, I'm convinced you can actually learn from the birds' songs. They really start talking when something's about to happen.

So, all these dynamics are at work, and I think some people have an intuitive sense of it, but they don't realize what it is, especially in their early years of fishing. They're focused on just catching fish and getting pictures and stuff, but there's value to what you can pick up by taking in the totality of being out there.

You're sort of an intermediary between the river and the expectations of it.

Yes. Visitors are very results oriented, and the results that they're looking for are fish. It's actually pretty stressful because the expectations don't tend to change from day to day, but the situation in which you're trying to fulfill them totally changes. So, we're often tempering that expectation.

How?

I have a saying: "You don't learn shit on a fifty-fish day." Because basically what happens is it's just *on*, but there's no challenge, and you don't really have to figure much out. It's when we work hard all day to catch ten—*that's* where a lot of the learning comes from. I try to remind people of that. "Think about your life. Most of your good learning came in the face of adversity, not in the easy successes. It's the same thing out here."

Is it different when you're out there on your own?

It can vary. Sometimes I'm like anybody else, like, "God dang, I just want to go down there and catch some fish." But for me, it's also a way to measure myself against the natural world. I think that's what human beings have been doing since they became, let's say, "conscious" or "self-aware." But it's funny because we're measuring the dynamic nature of human beings, and ourselves, against this thing that's not a yardstick—it's something way more fluid and amorphous. Time changes the relationship, too. No question.

It's amazing how you can know something so well and always be surprised.

It is. But I think some of the coolest relationships are some of the most unpredictable, right? Some really creative or spirited people—you can't box them in, and there's always that tension. Somebody wants to codify a relationship and the other person just wants to be free, and as long as they're free, they're themselves, and that's what you liked about them in the first place. It's kind of like that with the river, I think. You've got to accept it for what it is and embrace it—and just know that it's always going to be hard.

Then What?

Then you carve your journal up. Maybe a pink highlighter marks good titles, yellow are good verse lines, and orange are chorus concepts. Maybe you take all the good titles you have and compile them into a list of titles you can bring into a cowrite as a strong jumping-off point. (It's nice to feel prepared, even if you're crippled with anxiety in a writing room. At least you have some titles sitting there that you can reach for.)

Sometimes it's less logical. David Byrne wrote about the early filtration process of journaling in his book *How Music Works*:

> When some phrases, even if collected almost at random, begin to resonate together and appear to be talking about the same thing, it's tempting to claim they have a life of their own. The lyrics may have begun as gibberish, but often, though not always, a "story" in the broadest sense emerges. Emergent storytelling, one might say.

The Results of the Results

How can the process be codified and repeated so that we might just leave the art machine on twenty-four hours a day and have it crank out shiny little Hot Pockets of song? I don't think it works that way, at least not for me. All you can do is generate the raw material, then work it through the process and detach your ego from the finished product. That's a lot. But you can do it.

When I say "detach your ego from the finished product," here's an example of what I mean: My mother is an artist who has done a lot of sculpting in stone. An irony about working with stone is that it's a very obvious, hulking thing, and yet you never know exactly what you're working with. There are natural deposits that run through quarries and can discolor or weaken its properties. Stone carving is also a very dusty business; it can be difficult to see detail, so what you have to do is splash the stone occasionally with some water to clear the dust away. Mom had an idea to carve a bust of a reclining woman, and got a hunk of alabaster about the size of a healthy watermelon and went at it. After carving out the rough dimensions of the thrown-back head and exposed neck, she splashed the stone and revealed rose-red veins running through it—they now ran across the woman's face and down her neck, changing the sense of the piece entirely. Suddenly the questions were, "Has she been assaulted?" "Is her peaceful expression a comment on the pain she's been through?" "Is this political? Historical?" "Is she All Women?" "Is she Mother Earth?" And so on. None of this was in the original concept of the piece, but the raw material revealed a completely different energy.

I personally love when that happens. The medium wrestles back control from the artist's ego, and what arrives is a kind of compromise, or maybe it's a cease-fire that we refer to as "finished." When you get songs like that (and if you haven't, you will), you never forget it. You never forget splashing water on them and finding out what's staring back at you.

Journaling Jump-Starts

If you want to journal but don't know where to begin, here are some fuses for your firecracker brains. Refer to them. Scan them and cut them into strips and stick them around the house. Tape them to the bananas in your fruit bowl. Whatever gets you started.

- **What is your perfect workspace?** Describe it in detail running through each of the five senses. Is it indoor, outdoor, dark, light, sunny . . . by the beach, a ski slope, the fire escape, a graveyard? Are you drinking coffee, a smoothie, whiskey, water? Is it midnight, 5 a.m., high noon? See it, touch it, lick it, and report back.
- **What do you want a listener to get from your music?** And who is that listener, anyway? What do they look like? Where are they from? What are they doing while you're coming out of the speakers?
- **Pick a single object in front of you and write about it and only it.** If you're staring at a ketchup bottle thinking there

really isn't much to say about it, remember astronomer Carl Sagan's words: "If you wish to make an apple pie from scratch, you must first invent the universe."

- **Play "Verbs and Nouns."** Wilco lead singer Jeff Tweedy offers this exercise in *How to Write One Song*: in one column on a page, list ten verbs that have to do with a job or action—surfing, hammering, testing. In a second column, write out ten nouns within your range of vision—a cup of coffee, a book, the kitchen.

  Next: Draw lines to connect the verbs you chose with your nouns. Look for combinations you'd never have come up with on your own. Some will be duds at first, but play around with them until they conjure a fresh image, character, or scene. Maybe the rhythm in the words will spark a melody, but to be honest, I've tried this method, and it can just as easily spark a short story, a rant, or a home improvement idea. Doesn't matter—if you're jump-started, that's a win, and you'll have baked in what David Byrne calls "the pleasant ambiguity . . . [that] constitutes much of the reason we love music."

- **Let's say you had a "brand" as a writer, but you also had a pseudonym no one could ever trace back to you.** What would that alter ego sound like? Funny? Political? Ambient? Twangy? Emo? A three-hour loop of sneakers tumbling in a dryer? What if you gave yourself license to try it? Maybe just one song, for fun—just to see? What would it be about?

- **Three steps.** In an interview, songwriter Bernard Butler laid this plan out: (1) Write down something that happened, being as detailed and descriptive as possible. (2) Explain how it made you feel. (3) Describe where this experience has left you.

  You've basically just written the arc of a song: number one is your verses, number two is your pre-choruses, and number three is the chorus. That may sound fairly simplistic, but we're just getting you jump-started here. It's a seed, but it may grow into something.

- **If you're in a touring band: What song does your set need?** Is there a hole that you fill every night with a not-exactly-right song? Is it the opener? A closer? An anthem? Write about the kind of song that will make your show better. Start aiming that direction.
- **Song of the Week.** What's the best song you heard this week? What tipped you off to its greatness? What did it have this week that no other song had?

I won't swamp you with more of these because you could just do a search for "songwriting prompts" and spend the rest of eternity being prompted. But if one of these or just *part* of one gets you up and writing, then all of them have done their job. I hope they help.

Alt-Journaling and the Riff du Jour

There's an obvious problem with the method of journaling I just outlined: It's that some things don't come out in words. Things like, say, music.

"Journaling" doesn't strictly mean writing in a notebook. Eric Bazilian (founding member of the Hooters; cowriter with artists including Cyndi Lauper, Ricky Martin, and Carlos Santana; and writer of Joan Osborne's international smash, "One of Us") has an approach he calls "Riff du Jour."

What is Riff du Jour, exactly?

Riff du Jour is journaling, but it's unconscious journaling. I'll start singing words, and sometimes there's gibberish, but eventually a story emerges. And sometimes it's surprising. Sometimes it's scary.

How do you catalog all your Riffs du Jour?

I have phone recordings, and sometimes I'll go back and find one and use it for something, but generally I really have to capture the moment and then dive in and take it as far as it'll go. It's a mystical, magical, mysterious process that goes on, and I just have to be open to it and show up for work.

Which of your songs do you attribute specifically to Riff du Jour?

Every song I've ever written has been a Riff du Jour, just about. "One of Us," absolutely a Riff du Jour. "And We Danced" [the first major hit for the Hooters] was a notable exception. Rob [Hyman] and I were on a songwriting retreat for a week, and I said, "Hey, let's try to write a song totally from a melody. And these are the parameters: It's going to start before the downbeat, and it's going to develop from there."

So, you made up rules based on the downbeat?

That's sort of been my philosophy. There are three kinds of melodies: melodies that start on the downbeat, melodies that start *before* the downbeat, and melodies that start *after*. Melodies that start *after* it have become much more common in songwriting since this whole "track making" and "topline" [writing melodies on "top" of tracks] thing has happened because the track is leading the singer and the melody. The topline person hears a chord and says, "Okay, I'm going to react to that." With melodies that start ahead of the beat, the singer is taking control, and the band is following the singer. There is a sense of urgency if you're singing *into* the beat because you've got a story to tell and you can't wait to hear what the band is going to play. Interesting thing: Most Beatles songs? Before the beat. [*Sings*] "Oh, yeah I-I-I . . ." [*Sings*] "She loves you-u-u," and so on and so forth. "Yesterday" is on the beat. "All You Need Is Love" is after the beat, but he gets to keep that one. [*Laughs*]

Antennae Always Twitching

Former student Madison Emiko Love, who has worked with Selena Gomez, Lady Gaga, Ava Max, Camila Cabello, and others, has an ideating process that includes not just "being inspired" but also actively going out and hunting.

How do you search for song ideas?

I don't want to give away *all* my secrets, but I listen, read, and watch everything I can, old and new. I hear things at restaurants, on TV—especially hit television shows because they have some of the best writers working on those scripts. I scour the internet for quotes, old song titles that were popular from other decades, and then I make them my own in some way. I don't judge when an idea pops into my head, good or bad. If it's the stupidest idea ever, I laugh about it and write it down, no matter what.

An example of things I research: I was looking up a synonym for the word "unique," and I found the word "rare" in the list. I scribbled it down in the corner of the page in my notebook and went to a recording session for Selena Gomez. Three years later, "Rare" was a single and the title of her album. She even created a makeup company with Sephora called "Rare Beauty." So it's things like that—little concepts that turn into bigger things. You don't always know how powerful they can become. A song concept turns into an entire *album* concept *and* a message for young people everywhere.

How do you organize the bits and pieces you compile?

I have song journals that I've kept since college. I'm on book number 11. I have thousands of concepts that I jot down all the time. Sometimes I'll draw a huge picture, and then I'll write lyrics inside it with different-colored pens. I never use pencils because I don't like erasing anything. So, I always have a place to look for concepts. Or I'll open up my safe, look through my old journals, and see what I was thinking back then.

Did you just say "safe"?

[*Laughs*] Yeah. I put my journals in a safe. They're very precious! It's a fireproof safe, too.

When you're in a session, do you take a journal and just flip to any page and see what happens?

I always prepare myself. Like when I worked with Katy Perry, I spent the entire week before writing down about 700 concepts, and categorized them in case she wanted to write a breakup song that day, or something else . . . I only had two days writing with her, so I wanted to be 100 percent prepared and not caught off guard. I love to make sure I don't come to a session empty-handed. I'll have a chorus written or a bunch of ideas that I know are very strong.

Live Journaling

If these alternative methods don't feel immediate enough for you, you're not the only one. On the *Song Exploder* podcast, Grammy-nominated Philadelphia rapper Meek Mill and producer Don Cannon explained Meek's process while breaking down his song "Trauma":

Don Cannon: A lot of times when you write down things, you already got it—the feeling—out on paper. So now you're reading it back, and . . . it's very hard to give it the same energy.

Meek Mill: I make all my music on the spot. I don't write my music down, so as soon as I get a thought, I gotta rush to the booth and lay it down piece by piece.

The song *is* the journal in this case.

Conclusion

A through-line between these approaches is that songs come on like an emergency and can disappear as quickly. Writers are forever rushing out of rooms, rushing to instruments, rushing to microphones, all feverishly hitting the Record button to answer the call so they can capture it, sing it, rap it, play it, and, ultimately, share it.

Is one better than the other? You can't physically see me right now, but I'm giving you the Italian shrug—shoulders up, chin thrust forward, lips drawn clownishly downward, palms at shoulder height, turned skyward. It means, "Who knows?" Accept the not knowing—resign yourself to the fact that what's true and beautiful is also elusive.

Six

SILENCE

Keep returning to silence. It's God's first language, and everything else is a poor translation.

—Father Thomas Keating

Y ou've probably heard the phrase "music is the universal language." Well, it's not.

Even in the biggest arena shows, where thousands of fans are pumping their fists and screaming every word, it's hard to miss the security guys in their matching polo shirts, facing away from the stage like bored dads. They remind me that the subjectivity of art applies even to art I can't live without.

Music has *never* done the job of being universal, and in fact, it does the opposite. It groups subsections of people together; it's clannish; it accessorizes a particular aesthetic; it *excludes*. Writers antagonize each other via diss tracks. High schools have battles of the bands. TV networks pit musicians against each other in bizarre gladiatorial competition shows where contestants try to . . . what? Out-*music* one another? How can one speak in the universal language and still get kicked off the show?

So, what *is* universal? Thinking back to George Saunders's definition of art, the common element isn't the "undeniable and nontrivial" stuff that goes into the box—it's *the box itself.* Artists fill that box with color, sound, fireballs, foam, or whatever, but when the work ends, the box stills, and common denominators remain. So, what are those common denominators? What's inside the box when there's *nothing in the box*? What meets the songwriter before the first note is played?

Silence.

So, for the purposes of songwriting: *Silence is the universal language.*

If that's true, then *any note you play is a move away from universality.* Music chases universality away in the naive hope of creating something universal. It gets hard to avoid questions like: Has music helped us understand ourselves better than silence? Has it helped *me*? I'm not so sure. What I see in classes is that students' work is almost always improved by editing, which almost always means the elimination of parts of the song. *Adding more silence.* What I've concluded is that notes are nice and all, but *if you don't have something to say that improves on silence, then don't say it.*

Quiet Time

A distant memory: Me, in college, poking through the music stacks in the campus library. For some reason, I opened up a book by John Cage. Cage was writing about silence but leaving long gaps between the words and forcing that silence onto the page.

The gaps between the words became the whole point of the writing, and if that was the case, what the hell was I reading? And likewise, if silence could be a more compelling option than notes, a collection of only the best options would result in . . . a silent composition. Cage did this, of course, creating his famous piece, 4'33", to be performed—silently—for four minutes and thirty-three seconds. Was Cage getting out of the way of himself? Only offering the best choices? Making something close to perfect? Making us look like idiots?

Comedians have had fun with the idea of a silent piece, and I get it; on some level, it's insane, academic, elitist garbage. Cage knew that silence was impossible, anyway. Even in anechoic chambers, where all sound is canceled, he could hear his own body pumping blood past his eardrums; the beating in his chest; air whooshing past nostril hair, up through sinuses and into lungs. It was like Grand Central Station in there. Every performance of 4'33" is riddled with coughs and sneezes and door slams. But even that begs a question: Is *that* the piece? An interruption of the piece? An accompaniment?

That experience with silence has always felt more universal to me than charting out and examining, for example, the Beatles' "All You Need Is Love"—which, by the way, is false, unless you can eat it or sell it for food.

What I mean is: Maybe we already have it all, and our job is to lose as little of it as possible.

I believe in silence. It's where we came from and where we're going. As the universal language, it paves the way for any form of divinity to speak. It's countercultural. It awakens empathy. It reconfigures us.

So, Why Is Everyone So Afraid of It?

What does it contain that everyone is so adamant about drowning out?

Some experiments for you, laboratory-style: first, a theory; then, a test.

> **Silence is a fundamental truth.** Musicians strive for timeless, universal art, but the second they put a bow to a string or open their mouths, they stray from what is already timeless and universal and defeat their purpose.
> **How to test it:** Be quiet.

Silence is all we agree on. At the first sound, the first opinion of the sound arises, and following that first opinion, the first difference of opinion.

How to test it: Get in a heated argument about music. Afterward, notice what has been accomplished. Example: I ran the website for a big music magazine for a while, and our stated goal was to get people to argue about music. We chummed the internet with "listicles," which are lists pretending to be articles, and the more authoritative we made them sound, the more enraged readers got. When they argued, they engaged more and clicked around more, and the company sold more advertising. From the magazine's perspective, the argument *was* the win. The noise made money. Meanwhile, no one ever figured out the Top Ten Songs of Summer or the Top Ten Guitarists of All Time—or anything, really.

Silence is the universally empathetic moment in music. It connects us so powerfully that many of us can't bear it. We literally "break" the silence.

How to test it: Consider this quote from Blaise Pascal: "All of humanity's problems stem from man's inability to sit quietly in a room alone."

Silence is so awkward! Our resting state is a quiet one; noise is the attempt to escape it. Our culture thrives on noise; our economy depends on it. Meanwhile, true friends are people you can sit with in silence.

How to test it: Pick five friends and sit silently with each for twenty minutes. Then reassess your friendships.

Silence is consensual. One dissenter, and it's gone. Silence is a unanimous decision. When a community joins in, the (silent) result fulfills the same function as the chorus of a song.

How to test it: Go to a Quaker meeting. Consider what consensus of opinion entails.

Silence is free of cliché. As John Cage demonstrated, it's always different.

How to test it: Sit silently in three different rooms for twenty minutes. Notice the difference.

Silence is rebellion. Sometimes, it's the only way to be heard. From the "silent treatment" of childhood, to the silent protests of the Black Lives Matter movement, to the deletion of social media accounts, disengagement from sound is dissent. Silence is punk. It gives the middle finger to the noise we've created.

How to test it: Consider the fire-extinguishing system at Yale University's Beinecke Rare Book Library. The building, which is shock-mounted to resist earthquakes, also contains a large column into which the rarest books are placed. If there is a fire, instead of dousing the books with water or chemicals, which would destroy them, a fire-suppressing gas is emitted that lowers oxygen levels inside the column (without killing librarians). Apply this approach to your next confrontation. Instead of hosing it down, deprive it of oxygen. Save the rare books.

Silence is wise. Younger people fill a void; older people work with it. Performing musicians are hailed as having "restraint in later years." What they're doing is admitting—and allowing—silence. Sounds are important, but the silences around them reveal which ones have value. Silence is closer to the center of things.

How to test it: Choose an artist with a long career; notice the difference in early- and late-stage work. What are the choices being made, and how are they applicable to your own brief time here?

Silence is often the better choice.

How to test it: Take something and erase it.

Silence is genius. People who work alone are often misunderstood and ostracized by a "pack mentality" culture that is inherently threatened by them. Collaboration can be effective, but brainstorming sessions and think tanks can also drive maverick minds toward lukewarm compromise. Silence welcomes the opposite—idiosyncratic, unencumbered, and original solutions.

How to test it: Watch a movie alone. Notice where your opinions travel when relieved of the social obligation to "chat about it" afterward.

Silence is art. The Mute button on a recording console implies that something is being subtracted from a piece of music when in fact something universal is being added. In the way the Delete key is the writer's best friend, the Mute button—the choice to add silence—is the composer's. It works on song sections (say, cutting the intro) as well as on parts within those sections (muting the horns).

How to test it: Find musical examples where silence is used as the accelerator for a dramatic moment. Then take a song of yours and add some silence. Then assess.

Silence is medicine for the world. In her book *Quiet*, Susan Cain debunks the "catharsis hypothesis," which states that venting pent-up aggression—"letting off some steam"—is a healthy release. "Scores of studies show that venting doesn't soothe anger; it *fuels it*." Public discourse, social media in particular, is a place where that myth is exercised to disastrous effect. Social media's ability to react without introspection compounds "groupthink" feedback loops. Perhaps worst of all, those feedback loops are easily gamed by bad actors, with the result being the bending of the nature of truth itself.

How to test it: Suspend your social media accounts for one week. Assess your mental state. Repeat as needed.

Silence is the music that music dances to.

How to test it: Write something and see if it dances.

Seven

WHAT THE BRAIN LIKES

O ur audience is the human brain. Apologies to those who feel I'm giving the heart the short end of the stick here, but what can I tell you? Hearts can be transplanted. You know who figured out how to do that? Brains.

I'm not a neurologist, but as a songwriter, I've done some tinkering and a little market research, and here's what I've noticed:

The Brain Likes to Be Right

When the brain figures something out, it orders the arm to give a victorious little fist pump. We might emit a *Yesss* or look for someone to high-five. These gestures are the brain throwing itself a victory parade because that's how much it likes to be right. Also at the victory parade: dopamine, a neurotransmitter that opens the doors of the brain's reward and pleasure centers. The victory parade runs right through those doors, and it's a pretty kick-ass after-party.

Having gotten a taste of delicious dopamine, the brain becomes restless to repeat the process. Why? Maybe it's curious about the process, maybe it's hooked on dopamine—and maybe that's what curiosity is, which is a little depressing. Entrepreneurs identify the cycle (problem/solution/victory parade/search for more problems) and capitalize on it by inventing little obstacle courses for the brain to run: mobile games featuring bubbles that need organizing; Rubik's

Cubes; fantasy sports leagues; and so on. But it doesn't have to be that elaborate: even normal, everyday puzzles can give similar results. When the amps and guitars all fit in the trunk of the car? When dinner is comprised only of leftovers but actually tastes good? *Yesss.*

A song provides something similar: it's a puzzle with pieces we call *sections* and larger patterns we call *song form.* By learning the repeated twists and turns in the music, decoding the lyrics, and identifying the bigger picture it presents, the brain "solves" the puzzle the writer has created. Then? Victory parade. With dopamine.

There are a few basic song forms that have proven incredibly durable despite changing fashion trends and technological leaps. You can chart out songs that were released decades apart and see a similar logic in the same way building blueprints address the common laws of gravity. Why? Because the product (a song in one of these forms) still yields a reward (sweet, sweet dopamine). And when the product is successful, the reasonable conclusion is to continue creating the product.

There are three basic song forms. I won't dwell on them because this information is ubiquitous:

1. verse – verse – pre-chorus – chorus – verse – pre-chorus
   – chorus – bridge – chorus(es)
   (see Kelly Clarkson, "Since U Been Gone")
2. A section – A section – B section – A section – B section
   – A section
   (see the Beatles, "Yesterday")
3. A section – A section – A section – A section
   (see Tom Waits, "Walking Spanish")

Yes, there are more popular AAAA songs than Tom Waits's "Walking Spanish," but it's my book, and I like that song.

Please note: I'm being reductive in order to be clear. Of course, there are endless variations. Rappers in my classes can feel restrained by the forms I mentioned, and the reasons stem directly from the priorities of the art: many are telling linear stories that work like epic poems or novels. Novelists don't repeat key chapters, so why would a rapper? A chorus, from that perspective, is actually a speed bump in the story and an interruption in the plot. More pop-leaning rappers will toss the chorus to a singer, but some will argue that lyric and flow contain the larger meaning within the work; as a result, I get a lot of songs that, if you were to chart them, would read, simply, "A . . ." In these cases, I suggest they throw the brain a bone by putting some repeated information in the instrumental arrangement—a defining "hook" that a listener can sing back, thereby infecting the next potential fan. Hook recognition is a form of puzzle solving, which is a win-win: the writer keeps the intent of the art alive while writing in a language the listener can grasp.

Can the writer do absolutely *none* of these things and still make something beautiful and have people listen and live a wonderful, productive life? Yes. Of course, yes. Your audience for that kind of music would be me, actually, because I love a good eight-hour-long Max Richter concept album based on the human sleep cycle; I love a good cow choir on TikTok. I get tired of being spoon-fed choruses. Hell, I even get tired of pizza if I'm given enough of it. What I'm saying is that the Venn diagram of your listeners may vary—and, like your diet, maybe it should.

Yes, the Brain Likes to Be Right . . . but Not Consistently

A puzzle the brain can nail in a minute (e.g., a six-piece jigsaw of an owl on a branch) is mastered and quickly forgotten. Mobile games that are initially "addictive"—and notice that word—get boring. The thrill is gone. Satisfaction recedes, and the brain gives chase, searching for either more challenging, dopamine-rich puzzles or, failing that, cheaper and dirtier thrills. The best place to score that kind of junk is social media, with its likes, hearts, and follows. That's bottom-shelf dopamine and a lot of us are completely tweaked on it.

But just as the brain doesn't like puzzles that are too easy, it hates puzzles that are too hard. This is why so many popular puzzles are referred to as "brain *teasers*" and not "brain *embarrassers*." Inability to solve a puzzle means no dopamine, and that is not an acceptable result.

We want to strike a balance and write a song that meets expectations in unexpected ways—one that satisfies but not without a little work. We do that by giving recognizable forms, like the ones I just mentioned, and then running a few trick plays to keep us engaged. Social media algorithms do something very similar. In *Ten Arguments for Deleting Your Social Media Accounts Right Now*, scientist, musician, and tech writer Jaron Lanier says, "It's not that positive and negative feedback work, but that somewhat random or unpredictable feedback can be more engaging than perfect feedback. . . . It's as if your brain, a born pattern finder, can't resist the challenge." This brand of gamesmanship fuels addiction, whether it's to online poker, cryptocurrency speculation, or the song you can't get out of your head.

The Brain Likes Company

We are social animals, and we like to run in packs. We have matching team jerseys, matching leather biker jackets, and matching choruses in songs that serve pretty much the same function.

In the ancient sense of the word, "choruses" are, literally, packs of people, often in matching robes, who sing together. The dictionary doesn't even distinguish the chorus as a uniquely human activity; animals croak, tweet, squawk, and howl in packs, too.

Most choruses have matching lyrics that are repeated several times so they can be recognized and "solved"—in other words, remembered and successfully sung back—by the brain. A big, identifiable chorus, then, is not unlike a big, identifiable skull patch on a biker jacket: it's a recruiting tool to get other brains to "join" the gang of the song. There's even a term, "gang vocals," where a bunch of people sing the chorus together—Queen's epic "We Will Rock You" is a shining example of a song that knows how much the brain loves company.

A second benefit of membership in the "gang" of the song is that we get to align ourselves with the message of the lyric. Songs can put parts of our lives into words we can't find—and it can do so in an amplified way that draws a like-minded community together. We get the sense that we are not alone, which is a very powerful message for pack animals like us. Even when the music is bleak and alienating, it can bring arenas full of bleak and alienated people together in one big bleak, alienated army; the process seems counterintuitive if you're on the outside, but it's deeply consoling to those on the inside. We feel seen, and we are given words to express it. The song becomes a gathering place.

You might have heard people say that no one listens to the lyrics. In response, I would simply point to the charts, which is where "everyone" is doing the listening. How many instrumentals do you see in the Top 10? Top 40? 100? *200*? None? Maybe one every couple of years? Okay. If we are brains in search of patterns, that's a no-dopamine revelation. Keep looking: What are two of the most popular genres? Hip-hop and country. They live and die on lyrics, turns of phrase, and anthemic choruses. And that's not "my opinion." That's people showing their preferences. But seriously, did you even have to look? I mean, what do you think people tattoo all over their bodies? The horn charts?

Rule: Don't ever let someone tell you people don't listen to the lyrics. The facts simply don't support it.

Corollary: Don't skimp on your lyrics because you believe no one listens to them. They do.

The Brain Likes the Number Four

We love multiples of four: there are four-bar sections, the "middle eight," twelve-bar blues, sixteen-bar solos, thirty-two-bar song form, and the 4/4 time signature, in which a vast majority of pop music is written.

Why? Some say we pick it up by absorption via nursery rhymes and the pop music we grow up around. Some say it mirrors the physical rhythms of being bipeds or, further back, to what we felt in the womb as the offspring of bipedal mothers. (So, if we had three-legged mothers, we'd write more waltzes, I guess?) Somehow, in the cacophony that comprises us, four has won out, and our pop songs reflect that.

Like a poker player who spots a "tell" at the card table, a writer who recognizes the brain's bias can exploit it. Songs and sections can be destabilized by *avoiding* divisibility by four. Other time signatures can be introduced, phrases can run over bars to imply sections of different lengths, and the brain can generally be messed with before landing on stable, repeated sections it can join in on.

The questions, then, are solely artistic: Where on the line of solvability is the "puzzle" of your song? How satisfying will that dopamine deal with the listener be? How hard should they have to work for it? Will they be given the stability of four-bar phrases? Will the song be in a solid 4/4 time signature, loping 6/8, disconcerting 5/4? Weird combinations of all of them? And when they get a tattoo, what will it say?

The most important question remains: What will *your* song provide?

Eight

MISSION SONGS

If you're a Bruce Springsteen fan, you know that he's from New Jersey. If you've ever listened to Eminem, chances are excellent that you know he's from Detroit. You may know Kendrick Lamar is from Compton, Jennifer Lopez is from the Bronx, Pitbull is from Miami, and the North Mississippi Allstars are from . . .

How do you know where they're from? Because they told you—a million times. In song after song, they've created a world by planting signifying flags, both literal and metaphorical, in the hopes that you will identify with their artistic journey and want to be a part of it.

Let's call these musical flag plantings Mission Songs. If you've ever had to write a topic sentence for a paper or read the mission statement of a school or company, you're familiar with the concept. These songs lay out the story of the artist—what they believe in, where they're from, what they want. They're decoding glasses.

Since you're journaling now, you're hopefully getting closer to articulating what you're about, too. You're compiling clues in that notebook. If nothing massive and "profound" has arrived yet, don't despair. Missions aren't always world-shattering. Maybe while writing, you're feeling something more immediate: maybe you're all about the weekend, or all about going grocery shopping, or all about just getting more sleep, or—you get it. Whatever you stand for, big or small, if you resonate on a strong enough frequency and hold to it, then a listener can plug in and identify with you. And identifying with you is the first step toward liking you and becoming a fan.

Here's an example of a Mission Song success story, ripped from the pages of music history. You've heard of Kiss? With the makeup, the dragon boots, the breathing fire, and all that? Of course you have.

Picture this as a *songwriting* challenge: bassist Gene Simmons was a kabuki-inspired demon who'd pop blood capsules in his mouth and "bleed" all over his axe-shaped bass; guitarist Ace Frehley was "from space"; singer/guitarist Paul Stanley was vaguely described as a "star-child"; and drummer Peter Criss was (checks notes) a cat? This was a band that needed a musical decoder ring. But they didn't just need a great song; they needed a song that would *tell listeners what they were about*. Without it, they were a blur of blood, fire, boots, space people, cat drummers—all of which is great for a live show but confusing for a listener.

In 1974, Kiss's label, Casablanca Records, pulled them off the road, where they were touring behind the commercially sluggish album, *Hotter than Hell*. The head of the label, Neil Bogart, pushed writers Paul Stanley and Gene Simmons to find a song with a centering through-line that connected the many disparate dots. The model Bogart used was "I Want to Take You Higher," a funky, roaring Mission Song by Sly & the Family Stone. Sly had an *anthem*, and Kiss needed one, too.

"I was kind of taken aback," lead singer Paul Stanley told me over the phone. "'What do you mean by an anthem?' And Neil said, 'A song that your fans can rally behind. A song that says what you stand for and what the *manifesto* is.' I had seen Sly & the Family Stone when they first started out, opening for Hendrix at the Fillmore East, and, you know—Sly was a game changer. The metamorphosis of so many bands was based on [them]. So, I went back to our hotel and picked up my guitar."

While the goal was to write a Mission Song, Paul explained, "I wanted to make sure that the writing was never going to be pontificating. It would more be celebrating and mirroring what I was feeling rather than telling people what they should feel." Like Sly, he used the first-person point of view to accomplish that while generating a similar kind of immediacy. "When you pledge allegiance, it's not '*We* pledge allegiance'; it's not '*They* pledge . . .'; it's '*I* pledge allegiance.' So, instinctively, and without much thought, I went, '*I* want to rock and roll all night and party every day.' And [the chorus] went right back to it—it was incessant, and insistent. And with that, I went and knocked on Gene's door and said, 'What do you think of this?'" Gene Simmons stripped parts from another song, "Drive Me Wild." "[It] was perfect. The two married together without really any alteration . . . and then it was a matter of, 'How do you make this concise?'"

The result, "Rock and Roll All Nite," still didn't rocket up the charts *until* it was incorporated into the live show via their (fourth!) album, *Alive!* At that point, the song, plus the crowd reaction, assembled the pieces for listeners. "What people saw was this sense of empowerment and rebellious individuation . . . 'I want to rock and roll all night and party every day' encapsulated, in one sentence, what we were all feeling . . . once that was embraced, the band took off."

I asked Paul how many subsequent Kiss songs grew into anthems that the band couldn't leave the arena without playing. He laughed. "*All of them.* How about that?"

So, we're not in Kiss, but we're tasked with the same question: How do we define ourselves within songs that others can inhabit? How do we find something within ourselves that is both differentiating and inviting? How do we form a gang in song form? And how do we invite others in?

I've broken down some different categories of Mission Songs and tossed in some prompts, hoping to spark some ideas. As you read these, ask yourself, "If I were to write that kind of Mission Song, what would it be about? And what would it sound like?" You'll be asking yourself what kind of flag you can plant and what kind of artist you want your listeners to know you are. And, maybe it goes without saying, but you can have a bunch of Mission Songs; you can stand for a lot of things—including nothing. (Standing for nothing is a pretty popular stance, actually.)

You may roll your eyes at some of these titles, and I'm sure some of these songs will age poorly, but I'm not suggesting putting them on your party mix—I'm recommending you study what they did for the writers and artists who sang them.

Call to Action

These songs have titles with active verbs that address "you" directly. (Sly's "I Want to Take You Higher" fits here.) These are war cries, romantic invitations, or petty grievances—not everything is that deep. Examples: "Fight the Power," Public Enemy; "Come Away with Me," Norah Jones; "Call Me Maybe," Carly Rae Jepsen; "Say Something," A Great Big World; "Take Me to Church," Hozier; "Take a Bow," Rihanna; "Shake It Off," Taylor Swift; "Pump Up the Jam," Technotronic; "Kiss Me," Sixpence None the Richer; (Get in) "Formation," Beyoncé; "Lean on Me," Bill Withers; "Take This Job and Shove It," Johnny Paycheck; "Cover Me Up," Jason Isbell; "Work It," Missy Elliott; "Let It Be," the Beatles; "Let It Go," *Frozen*; "Know Yourself," Drake; "Shut Up Kiss Me," Angel Olsen; "(You Gotta) Fight for Your Right (to Party!)," the Beastie Boys; and so on. Often, you'll see the active verb pushing the agenda right there in the title, before the first note is played.

The payoff for the listener is that they get to inhabit a desire and wear it publicly. Isn't that a cool part of this job—to give people the means to express themselves? What a gift writers, and songwriters in particular, have, because they also get to animate those words via melody, timbre, and attitude.

Here's a prompt: Find a verb, put it in the imperative mood, and give us an anthem, big or small, for the arena or the bedroom.

Mindset

The world has no idea who you are, and it's your job to tell them. One of the most effective examples of this I've ever seen is Eminem's "My Name Is." In the video, he literally knocks on the inside of the TV set, as if interrupting popular culture, and announces, "Hi! My name is/my name is/my name is . . . Slim Shady." He then goes on an epic tear, defining himself, his upbringing, his goals ("to piss the world off"), and by the end of that song, you've either bought in or not. Either way you went on Em, it wasn't for lack of information.

This kind of Mission Song answers the question, "What are you all about?" In the Smiths' "How Soon Is Now?" Morrissey sings, "I'm the son and the heir of a shyness that is criminally vulgar." From that galvanizing line, not only do we get a mindset, but we also get a trove of place-based information; is there any doubt that someone from the United Kingdom wrote a line like *that*? Similarly, if you're in the Beatles and you're tired of being told who you are, you write an absurdist, personality-driven Mission Song like "I Am the Walrus" and put a stick in the listener's eye.

Other titles that relate an idea that you can embody: (I'm the) "Man in Black," Johnny Cash; (I'm the) "Bad Guy," Billie Eilish; (I'm) "Mr. Brightside," the Killers; "I'm Every Woman," Chaka Khan; (I'm a) "Savage," Megan Thee Stallion; "I'm a Believer," Neil Diamond/the Monkees/Smash Mouth; "I Am a Man of Constant Sorrow" (traditional); (I feel just like a) "Rockstar," Post Malone; "I'm the Only One," Melissa Etheridge; (I'm a) "Loser," Beck; "I Am a God," Kanye West; (I am) "Doll Parts," Hole; "I Am Yours," Andy Grammer; (I'm a) "Creep," Radiohead; "I'm a Mess," Bebe Rexha; (I'm just a) "Teenage Dirtbag," Wheatus; and so on.

Here's a prompt: What are you about *that I can also be about*? Tell us what that is, even if it's what you're about for this moment. Plant a flag—genuine, sarcastic, metaphoric—and run with it. "I am ____." It might sound ridiculously easy to you, but committing to a Mission Statement is brave, and bravery is its own reward. The simple act of confession is cathartic.

Destiny

These songs establish a backstory that grounds the artist in an aura of inevitability. They say, "Something about me is *predetermined*. It is beyond my control; it is beyond *all of our control*. Fate has spoken, and here I am." The word "born" is big in these kinds of songs: "Born This Way," Lady Gaga; "Born to Run," Bruce Springsteen; "Born in the U.S.A.," Bruce Springsteen, again (hmm, interesting); "Born to Die," Lana Del Rey; "Born Here Live Here Die Here," Luke Bryan; "Born to Be Brave," *High School Musical*; "Born to Be Yours," Kygo/Imagine Dragons; "Born Country," Alabama; "Born under a Bad Sign," Albert King—I mean, it's endless. And for good reason.

Here's a prompt: What are you born to do? What is your *birthright*, real or imagined? Describe it, your reaction to it, and your plan on navigating it—including escaping it. (No one says you have to love what you were born into. Some of Springsteen's biggest songs are about being born to run *away from* New Jersey—and Jerseyites *eat it up.*)

Place

This might be the easiest one to spot, and we went over it a little bit already, but you can imagine how Alicia Keys singing, "Let's hear it for New York!" plays in New York. These flag-planting anthems can be literal—a city, state, or country—but they can also call out a metaphorical place: the Heartland, the boondocks, "God's Country." A personal favorite of mine is in Kacey Musgraves's "Merry Go 'Round," in which she connects to her listeners with the deceptively simple phrase "same trailer, different park." I'm reminded of a Korean American friend who once said to me, "Korean, Italian, you know . . . same noodles, different sauce." I appreciate attempts like these to connect us to one another, and place-based Mission Songs have the power to do that.

Here's a prompt: Where are you from, literally or metaphorically? Take a trip around town and tell us what it's like. Will we find part of ourselves in it? Will we find part of ourselves in *you*?

Universality

Here's where you get to speak for the masses, whoever they are. The personal pronoun "we" establishes the mission of a group and presumably puts you in the role of that group's ambassador. When Kurt Cobain wailed, "Here we are now, entertain us," in Nirvana's "Smells Like Teen Spirit," a generation was able to resonate in a brief unison around the band's sarcastic, nihilistic fury. ("Teen Spirit," if you didn't know, was the name of a popular deodorant marketed to teen girls.)

Other examples: "We Are the World," U.S.A. for Africa; "We Are Young," fun.; (We'll never be) "Royals," Lorde; (We can be) "Heroes," David Bowie; "We Shall Overcome," Pete Seeger; "This Is How We Do It," Montell Jordan; "We Are Bulletproof: The Eternal," BTS; "We Are Family," Sister Sledge; (We're gonna) "Rock Around the Clock," Bill Haley & His Comets; "We Are the Champions," Queen.

Here's a prompt: Write "us" an anthem. What are "we" all in agreement on?

Mission of Mission

Don't get me wrong: songs don't necessarily *need* to be about any-thing, and neither do Mission Songs. I never thought I'd say this, but, consider "Boom Boom Pow" by Black Eyed Peas:

> *Boom boom boom*
> (repeat)

Or "All Together Now" by the Beatles:

> *All together now*
> (repeat)

Or one of my favorites, "Everybody Everybody," by the 1990s group Black Box:

> *Everybody everybody*
> (repeat)

These are fantastic because there's nothing to argue against; there is only inclusion. The song's mission is both undefined and irrefutable. How great is that?

People who look at lyrics like this on the page and conclude that they're "stupid" don't really understand their function. Remember, a lot of what makes music work in practice doesn't look like much on the page.

Consider:

Palm Mute

The sweat, power, and glory of that, when blasted out of a Marshall amp, is *not* on the page.

The written instructions for sexual intercourse suffer the same basic problem.

Here's a prompt: Get away from the constraints of language, and stop making sense. Find a productively ambiguous rallying cry. Bring us all in for a hokey-pokey of the subconscious mind. Freak us out!

Extensions of Mission Songwriting

Once you have a Mission Song draft with a strong point of view, you can recast it in different ways to vary your points of view. Here are a couple of ideas to consider:

Change the Personal Pronoun

He's the bad guy; *she* was born to run—this adds a new character and creates a *story song* with the opportunity for narrative *and* the energy that a Mission Song can generate. Instead of *you* standing for something, your characters do, and they can move through a scenario in a decisive and intriguing direction. (You can also have them live out the consequences of a mission by rewarding them or killing them off, which can be instructional—and fun!)

Here's a prompt: Take a Mission Song, change the personal pronoun, and send that character on a journey.

Get Conditional

I've made a bit of a stink about how *decisive* a Mission Song can be and how clear a path it can carve, but what if that doesn't work for you? What if you wish you were on a mission but you're vulnerable, fragile, scared, insecure, or just unsure what's next in your life? You can express that kind of energized instability by adding a conditional phrase to the title or centering lyric: *If* I were born to run, I ——; *If* you would just ——; *If* he/she/they ——; *If* we ——; and so on. Taylor Swift does this to great effect on "the 1" as she grudgingly accepts a possible romantic outcome that, alas, has not come to pass: "It would've been fun / If you would've been the one."

Here's a prompt: Take a Mission Song and add *if*. Bonus prompt: Add *if* and change the personal pronoun in order to create the energized story of an unstable character. "If she saw ——," "If he were a god, ——."

Your Mission: Destroy a Mission

When Courtney Love sings, "I am . . . doll parts . . . ," you get the sense that (1) she's not, and that (2) the Destroy Feminine Stereotypes button has been smashed. As a writer, you can bend a political or social mission by naming it or by sarcastically following it to its logical absurdity—a rhetorical device called *reductio ad absurdum* that dates back to Greek philosophy and has stayed relevant because it's just so damn fun to write. Parody songs use this tactic a lot; when the Lonely Island yells, "I'm on a boat!" the butt of the joke is someone who'd say exactly that.

Here's a prompt: Find a social norm or an expectation that is placed on you and explode it in a spectacular way that inspires others to do the same.

Your Mission Song Dartboard

If you feel like you have a flag but don't know where to plant it, maybe this will help. It's a game, kind of. One way to play it is to scan this page and tape it to a corkboard—and just throw a dart. Another way is to cut these slices up and put them in a hat so you can pick one out at random. Or skip the arts and crafts and just close your eyes and point at the page. Whatever you land on is your next song prompt. You'll find a way into a Mission Song that works. Be brave! I have faith in you!

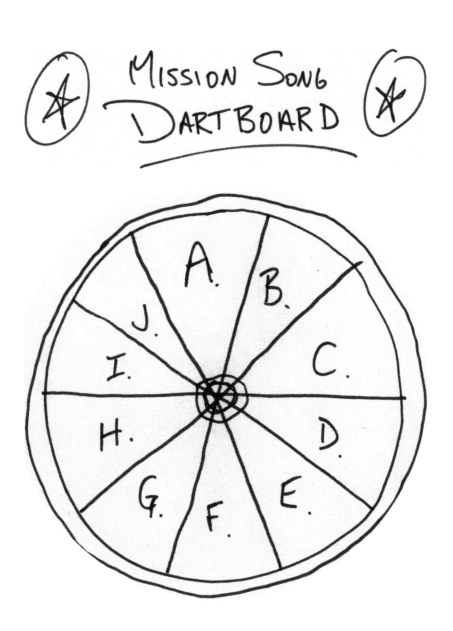

KEY

A. CALL TO ACTION : Find an action verb in direct address and go with it: "Fight The Power," "Take Me to Church," "Let It Go"

B. PERSONAL STATEMENT : Strike a pose- genuine or not - & describe it: (I'm The) "Bad Guy," "I'm Every Woman," "My Humels"

C. DESTINY : What are you born to do: "Born to Run," "Born this Way," "Born to Die." Describe it, & how you plan to navigate it.

D. PLACE : Where are you from, geographically, or metaphorically? Take us there: Compton, New Jersey, The Heartland, "some trailer, different park..."

E. MINDSET : What do you stand for, whether it's for life, or just for the morning? "I'm the Man in Black," "I Am the Walrus"

F. UNIVERSALITY : Write "us" on anthem: "We Are Young." (We'll never be) "Royals," "Here We are now, entertain us..." "WE ARE THE CHAMPIONS!"

G. MISSION OF MISSION : Make no logical sense, & find a productively ambiguous rallying cry: "Everybody Everybody"

H. TAKE A WALK — COME BACK LATER

I TAKE A MISSION, ADD "IF": Make a hypothetical call to arms using any personal pronoun: If I; If we; If they...

J. Your MISSION: DESTROY ALL MISSIONS : Refute a social or political stance, overtly or sarcastically; follow a stupid mission to its logical absurdity— We are ALL Royals; "Born to Rot," etc.

∗ BULL'S EYE: TAKE IN SOME ART — COME BACK LATER

Note: I'm serious about the "Take a Walk" and "Take in Some Art" sections, as you'll see later. Both can inspire as much as—or more than—the options that surround it. The only thing that definitely doesn't work is if you don't do anything.

Nine

THE QUADRANTS OF TRUST

Sooner or later, you're going to write about relationships. Most of us do.

Assumption: Relationships are built on trust, and trust is tricky. Fluid. With trust, a relationship can withstand temptation, boredom, distance, and whatever else life throws at it. Without trust, nothing of substance can grow—which, you know, isn't the worst thing, nor is it the worst thing to write about. There are persuasive arguments for surface relationships, one-night stands, arm's-length love, trial periods where maybe you're coming off something big and just need a minute to get back on your feet—all the colors of the relationship rainbow. All great song ideas. Each vantage point works. When you shake the tree, any one of these may fall out. If so, good.

Our job as songwriters isn't necessarily to figure out how to make a relationship work, thank God. Instead, we get to shine a light on where it might go, how great/not great it is, whether you are/aren't putting the effort in or tanking the whole enterprise—intentionally or not—and to offer what we find to the people who need it.

So, which vantage point are you going to pick? Maybe you're already bursting with ideas, and if so, great. If you need a push, let me give you something my dad gave me. It's a tool.

I doubt he made this up, and I don't know where he got it. My only clue is that he loved a guy named W. Edwards Deming, a management guru who helped reorganize the Japanese auto industry after World War II. Deming loved thought trees and pie charts. Logic. Order. The Japanese did well to listen to him. They made some good cars.

Here's the story: Dad noticed I was having trouble with relationships. I was a pretty sensitive guy traveling in some not-so-sensitive circles, and I was getting knocked around a lot. Dad listened as I told him and Mom about ugly breakups and ruined vacations, but no matter how one-sided I made the stories—and I goosed some details, I admit—he never really sympathized.

The women weren't the problem. The problem was that I didn't have a *process* that would yield the result I wanted. So my dad gave me one, and it turns out, you can apply it to songwriting, collaborating, hiring, marrying, or reorganizing the Japanese auto industry. Whatever. It's a multipurpose tool—my favorite kind. He called it the "Quadrants of Trust."

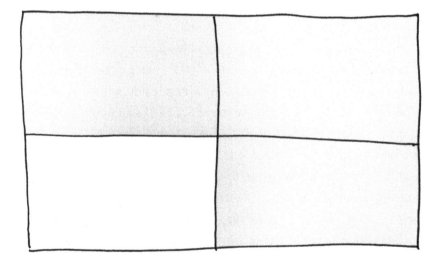

Top Left Quadrant: "I Trust You/You Are Trustworthy."

Obviously, this sounds like a good place to be. With mutual trust, progress has a foundation to build on. Everything becomes possible. The songs written in here are expressions of joy and gratitude, endlessly new ways to say, "I love you, you love me." (Barney the Dinosaur qualifies for this Quadrant, and, by the way, writing music isn't only about writing *pop* music for the jaded. Children's music is an evergreen market that allows a tremendous amount of arranging possibility, and you don't know where your career is going to lead you, so stay open to that possibility. If Stevie Wonder sang with the Muppets on *Sesame Street*, you should be so lucky to do the same.)

A drawback of this Quadrant is that it lacks *conflict*, and art without some kind of conflict has no gas in the tank and nowhere important to go. Nobody *wants* anything because they already *have* it. Compelling characters have to *want* something, and the best way to see what it is and how badly they want it is to put an obstacle in the way. As we already discussed in the section on the brain, overcoming obstacles is one of our favorite pastimes.

To achieve that, writers pull in conflict from nearby emotional real estate. Example: There's a song from the 1970s, "Reunited," with the lyric, "We both are so excited, 'cause we're REUNITED . . ."

Peaches & Herb—yes, that was their name, it was the 1970s—don't go deep into *why* they were apart, because that's not the point. They also don't articulate what brought them back together. (Maybe the couples therapy worked? Maybe he's out of the coma?) The point is, they are in that Top Left Quadrant because they *earned it back*. They deserve the joy they're feeling, and the song is their hard-won victory lap. Now, instead of Peaches & Herb's happiness coming off as gloating, the opposite occurs: their joy becomes something to aspire to. Rihanna's 2011 hit "We Found Love" sets up a similar dynamic in its hook, "We found love *in a hopeless place.*" In each song, some form of resistance has been introduced and overcome. Emotionally, this is like scooping up a basket of mewling kittens out of a burning building. Heroic! Joyful! It's a Top Left Quadrant emotion, but it's also an *earned victory* based on a condition that allows us to love it unconditionally.

Maybe you've got a few songs like that? Or maybe you have a sappy melodramatic song you can toughen up by adding a conflict you can resolve? That's having your cake and eating it, too—that kind of cake just tastes better.

Bottom Left Quadrant: "I Do Not Trust You/ You Are Not Trustworthy."

Nothing can grow here. "I think you're a jerk, you think I'm a jerk," nobody trusts anybody. To some, maybe that's titillating? Shocking and bottomless? Thrillingly noir and desolate? There are songs in here, though just as *everything's perfect* will earn you eye rolls, so will *everything sucks*. It's equally indulgent. There just aren't any stakes.

Again, pulling from other emotional territory provides a little traction. Adjacent to "Everything sucks" is, "Everything sucks, *but* underneath the black metal makeup, I just wish my parents understood me, and school wasn't so lame, and the world was a better place." That's not nihilism anymore. That's depression, disappointment, thwarted idealism—*the hope for something better*. If we inject hope, no matter how faint, into a song in this Quadrant, we introduce the stakes and hint at the distance between *what is* and *what would be a million times better*. The listener learns what the character *really* wants and gets an opportunity to empathize with, or even inhabit, that desire. A song like this is medicinal; it can function like a mirror for truths too raw to admit. We, as songwriters, can give the listener a chance to sing those truths out loud.

It's a long trip from this Quadrant to the top left (*I trust you/you are trustworthy*), but without a little hope, you might as well lie in a coffin and ask the world to shut the lid.

Top Right Quadrant: "I Trust You/ You Are *Not* Trustworthy."

I TRUST YOU/ YOU ARE TRUSTWORTHY | I TRUST YOU/ YOU ARE NOT TRUSTWORTHY

I DO NOT TRUST YOU/ YOU ARE NOT TRUSTWORTHY |

This is the house of broken hearts. Here are the notebooks swollen with tear-stained poetry. The ache of minor keys. This is the blues, of any shade. Torch songs, cry-in-your-beer songs. Angry-you-screwed-me-over songs. So. Many. *Songs.* Why? Because the stakes are right there in the name, and so is the failure.

Chances are you've been here, and chances are you'll be back. But here's the incredible thing: It's an *honorable place.* In this Quadrant, we've taken a chance—"I trust you"—and that's *brave.* We respect bravery. But more than that, it's *smart*. Why? Because "I trust you" is half of the ultimate, Top Left Quadrant (*I trust you/you are trustworthy*), and *it's the only part of that equation that's in your control.*

Meanwhile, you are avoiding the Quadrant you definitely do not want to visit:

Bottom Right Quadrant: "I Do *Not* Trust You/ You *Are* Trustworthy."

I TRUST YOU / YOU ARE TRUSTWORTHY	I TRUST YOU / YOU ARE <u>NOT</u> TRUSTWORTHY
I DO <u>NOT</u> TRUST YOU / YOU ARE <u>NOT</u> TRUSTWORTHY	I DO <u>NOT</u> TRUST YOU / YOU ARE TRUSTWORTHY

In this Quadrant, the conversation is not "I tried and I failed" but rather "I had it all, and I blew it." That, my friends, is hell on earth.

Are there songs in here? Oh, yes. Trapped, moaning, no-one-to-blame-but-myself songs. In the present tense, the songs are about fear: "You're the one, but I can't get out of my own way." In the past tense, they writhe with regret: "You were the one, and now you're gone. *I was such an idiot!*"

When I say, "You don't want to visit this Quadrant," I mean you as a *person*, not you as a writer. And here's a moment to discuss the difference between the two.

Maybe you think the way to know each of these Quadrants is to *live* your way through them. Maybe you're also seeing someone because it's "good material." Maybe you're dabbling in drugs because your heroes did. My advice is to relieve yourself of the myth of the broken artist. You don't need to suffer to get to work.

George Lucas didn't have to go to space to create *Star Wars*. No one's ever seen a hobbit. Hogwarts isn't on the map. That didn't stop the writing process, and it doesn't stop your audience's listening process. Let positive examples of imagination supplant negative examples of annihilation. Losing the love of your life for good material is a bad trade. Getting hooked on something because a hero did—I realize you didn't necessarily come to this book looking for life advice, but writing advice tends to jump the divider, now and then.

Conclusion

Take a look at your catalog through the lens of the Quadrants. Are you hanging out in one more than the others? Is there a reason? *Journal about that reason.* Squeeze it. Put that reason under the microscope and examine its details. Some say we spend our lives writing versions of the same few songs, as if they're echoes that emanate from a few central, defining wounds. Maybe, by examining your writing, you can identify those wounds and push out from them into new emotional territory. And maybe that'll help more than just your songs.

Ten

BLUE

So, how's your story going to sound? What tonalities are you going to use? What's going to work for this emotion? Or, if you're approaching the song from the opposite direction, what emotion is going to inspire a melody that will eventually carry language along with it? One of the roots of your answer will incorporate a fundamental pop music tool: the blues. But what does it mean when something sounds "bluesy"? When we reach for blue notes, or "blue" tonalities, what are we actually reaching *for*?

I'm white, from Brooklyn, of southern Italian descent—both sides of the family. I mention this up front because "blues" is a term that is historically associated with the Black experience in America. But the more I've worked with different musicians, the more I've come to understand this thing we call "blue" as a musical gesture found across all cultures.

To understand why a piece of music might feel "blue," let's back up—*all the way up*—to a definition of what sound is.

Music used to be a branch of physics, and you might know from physics class that sound is a spectrum of waves that move through a range of frequencies, high to low—high frequency, high notes; low frequency, low notes.

It's not unlike light, which moves through the range of colors, from red to violet. In the same way our eyes can't perceive the entire range of light—we just don't have the tools for that—our ears can pick up only a slice of the total range of sonic frequencies. There are highs that only dogs can hear, lows that whales can hear, and all kinds of crazy stuff in the universe that we've built cosmic wave-gathering instruments to detect. So, what we really have is a small window into this frequency range called sound.

Okay, physics class is over. All we needed to know is that there's some math involved. But we also know that people just love to mess with math. Different cultures have broken this band of sound waves into steps, known as notes. It's like the way Crayola picks a point along the spectrum of visible light and makes a crayon they'll call "Razzmatazz" or "Mango Tango."

In the Western tradition, the piano has twelve of these steps that cover the span of an "octave," which is a natural mathematical point where one pitch is twice the frequency of the other. As tidy as that sounds, there are different ways to "tune," or determine, those twelve steps. Meanwhile, some Arabic scales have twenty-four notes per octave, some ancient scales have only five, and from there, you're pretty much off to the races as to how you break up the octave into what we call "scales." What's interesting—to me, anyway—is how a "scale" varies from culture to culture, even though the range of sound available to us—the raw material of all this—remains fixed.

A "blue note" is more elusive than all this subdividing because, from what I've gathered in my experience, "blue" is about *context*. These sounds exist in the distances—and in the *journeys*—between scale tones, and they give music the ache that makes us scrunch up our faces and reach skyward. In their placelessness they plead for something beyond understanding and take us where words can't reach. Sweet, tortured, transcendent—despite the physical symptoms they induce in us, "blue notes" remain elusive.

Using the Western, twelve-tone approach, "blue notes" are most commonly a lowered third, fifth, or seventh. In some cases, they're technically "wrong notes" in that they don't belong in a given key, but it's common knowledge among musicians that any sound can work in any context if the artist handles the context right. Blue notes are most easily achieved with fretless instruments that allow for all the colors between given notes—the human voice is the best example, but the violin, viola, and cello do a great job of it. On fretted instruments, like guitars, notes are bent to get in between the scale tones. Some blues guitarists place a short glass or metal pipe, called a slide, on a finger of the fretting hand, negating the frets along the guitar neck and allowing for greater pitch flexibility. Sax and harmonica players bend the reeds with their breath. Even modern keyboards have a "pitch wheel" that allows for all the variety between keyed notes.

Examples of this achy, bluesy grind are everywhere in American blues and jazz and everything that comes after, obviously. But I can hear it in koto music too, with its contrast between clear scale tones and swooping bends that pass between them. I would even argue that silence—the act of spotlighting a note as it loses energy and "decays" in volume—is a harmonic choice that grinds against established scale tones. Silence, to me, can be unbearably blue. I hear blue everywhere, as if art, by proclaiming a unifying humanity, also casts a unifying shadow.

But Why Do We Call It "Blue"?

I've always felt a disconnect between blue the *color* and blue the *music*. To me, blue is just as easily associated with clarity, imagination, or space, with undertones of calm and peace. I mean—the cloudless sky! My childhood bedroom walls were sky blue, which was supposed to promote well-being (while doubling as a superhetero gender stamp). My point: "Blue" can mean a lot of things, including things that contradict one another. So what happened?

Interpretations of blue as "sad" date back centuries, to when the color was associated with sickness and death. The logic was pretty straightforward: if a person's body *actually looked blue*, they were in bad shape, especially considering what was passing for medicine back then—they had leeches, hammers, and wizards. Honestly, I don't know how we made it this far.

Examples of blue used as an *emotional* state show up as early as 1385 in Chaucer's poem "The Complaint of Mars." In short: Mars, the god of war, and Venus, the (married) goddess of love, attempt to have an affair, but it gets botched by Phoebus, the god of the sun, who shines his light on their shenanigans, making it impossible for them to ever see each other again. Understandably, Mars is pissed, and he crawls across the heavens complaining, "with tears blue and with a wounded heart." In ranting about how love and fate can make a living hell of man's time on Earth, Mars is basically singing a tortured, celestial version of the blues.

Fast-forward several hundred years, and the word becomes convoluted by music industry marketing. In the late 1940s, Jerry Wexler, a *Billboard* writer—who later moved to Atlantic Records and became a major force in defining pop music by signing acts including Ray Charles, Aretha Franklin, Led Zeppelin, and many others—coined the term "rhythm and blues," or "R&B," to replace the then-used term "race music." In effect, R&B became a blanket genre for Black artists, and the convention stuck. This skews our sense of what "blue" actually means. After a while, Wexler himself wasn't all that into it: he later regretted not calling it "rhythm and gospel" because so many of the elements of gospel are the ones that later translated to pop music, from the group singing, to the hand claps, to the many stars that came directly out of the church, including Sam Cooke, Sister Rosetta Tharpe, and Al Green.

This interpretation of the word "blue" is capitalism in action, and the logic is pretty simple: Originality is hard to sell, so businesses make it easier by creating buckets that define their product. Musical genres with catchy names like "R&B" function as those buckets, and when one bucket gets hot, copycat artists try to fill it with more stuff people will buy. Sometimes this means fudging genre labels and passing mimicry off as the real thing. Fakes slip through the cracks, and some of them get rewarded by a public that, let's face it, doesn't always know what it's buying. But capitalism is not the only culprit. To an ambitious artist, those popular buckets with all the money in them start to look like targets, and they start aiming. (We'll delve into this in Chapter 12.) This is where things get dicey, and this is where it gets relevant to us as songwriters.

Maybe you know what I mean when I say that some artists have an odd smell to them. They're talented, versatile, possibly child stars from TV shows or the Disney machine. They're scrubbed clean for a few seasons, cracking wholesome jokes and taking shaving cream pies in the face. So cute! But then, a few short media cycles later, they're back, and they're swaggering, flipping off cameras, and being a Mouseketeer's worst nightmare. All their endearing tells have changed overnight! Their origin stories! Their idioms! Their scales! What happened? It's like they had a cultural lobotomy, and a new history was implanted that—coincidence!—is very hot this season. Capitalism has a word for it: the "rebrand."

Ugly questions can—and should—be asked in this moment, but one I return to is, "Why tell someone else's story when there are so many of our own available, right there, between the notes?"

I'm not going to point fingers, and I'm not going to claim to be innocent because to a (much) lesser degree, this has happened to me in my time in the music industry. Although a wide range of artists influenced my writing, I was stamped and sent to market as "Dave Matthews meets Stevie Wonder." I know, I know. The Venn diagram does not offer a ton of overlap. What can I tell you? Their names, meant to focus me in the market, actually smeared the lens. The question I was too naive to ask at the time was, "So where are *your* stories, Mike? Where is *your* blues?"

My label arranged a meeting with Ben Mink, a producer I'd fallen in love with through his collaboration with country-torch singer k.d. lang. In k.d.'s recordings, I heard the clear influence of Patsy Cline, but also a kind of mourning I couldn't place. Her voice swooped in and around the melodies, but so did the pedal steel guitar and the violins and fretless bass parts, each in ways that introduced an interpretation of that word "blue" that was foreign to me.

Turns out, Ben's parents were Eastern European Jews who fled to North America with an ingrained knowledge of liturgical, folk, and Yiddish theater music. Later on, Ben got deep into klezmer music, which, if you're listening for it, is embedded in the fabric of American pop music. He told me that Louis Armstrong lived with a religious Jewish family as a kid, and he introduced me to recordings like "Black and Blue," a song that mixes some pretty obvious klezmer licks into Armstrong's New Orleans blues melodies. This is more or less what Ben did with k.d. lang, and the result of their work feels original to the two of them and, by some idiosyncratic definition, bluesy.

While Ben and I were together, we decided to cowrite a song. I had lyrics, and some musical ideas worked out, but we needed a melodic line to glue the arrangement together. Ben tasked me with finding that line, and in a Vancouver hotel room, I reached into my Stevie Wonder bag—I actually had no Dave Matthews bag—and coughed up what probably sounded like a discarded background vocal from *Innervisions*.

Ben listened to what I'd come up with, then paused and asked, "Where are your people from? I mean, before Brooklyn." I told him they were southern Italian, and he asked if I had any connection to that tradition. I told him there's a mandolin with worn-out frets on my parents' mantel that my Neapolitan great-uncle used to play; that my grandmother was an opera singer; and that this kind of music reverberated through my childhood. Ben brought up people like Enrico Caruso and Ennio Morricone and told me to look there for answers and skip the Stevie thing. I did, and the result was a song called "1000 Miles," with mournful violin lines played by Ben. It's a song that touches me in a way very few of my other songs can, but I couldn't possibly tell you why. I just picture my grandmother, with her eyes closed and her arms outstretched, giving it the desolate lilt that only diva opera singers can manage. It may pass over other ears, but I can hear my story and how that story connects to Ben's. I really hope you can write a song like that for yourself because it's satisfying in a deep and primal way.

For Your Consideration

I'll ask the same big "blue" question that was asked of me: What is *your* "blues"? Where are you looking? Are you paraphrasing what's already been said, or are you finding a way into your own story of what it means to you to be alive? More specifically, what is *uniquely yours* now that you're writing about what is *universally ours*?

Our cultures and ancestors are on the tips of our tongues every time we open our mouths. In each dimension of a song—lyric, melody, rhythm—there they are, speaking through us. I often wonder how much conscious choice we're even making and to what extent we're passive receptors of an origin story that echoes through our hands and voices. There's no such thing as being alone while writing.

That may sound like a dramatic way of putting it, but these are the stakes involved when you ask people for their time and attention. You owe it to them to have done the work.

Infinity, and Stuff

Raul Midón began his career as a session musician for artists including Shakira, Julio Iglesias, and Little Louie Vega. His debut, *State of Mind* (Manhattan Records), was released in 2005, and a string of recordings have followed, including *A World Within a World*, *Synthesis*, and *Bad Ass and Blind*. (Born prematurely, Raul and his twin brother Marco were blinded in an incubator without proper eye protection.) He has been nominated for two Grammy Awards and has collaborated with legends like Bill Withers, Herbie Hancock, and Stevie Wonder. Originally marketed as a pop act, both he and the category have undergone numerous reinventions. We talked about what's between the notes, the beats, and the genres.

Where are you from?

New Mexico. But my dad is from Argentina, so Argentine folk music is something that I tap into. I think one of the things happening now is that we have music all over the world, and everybody's influenced by everything, and yet we still have these silos of music. When I go somewhere, I don't want to hear their pop music or bands that sound like U2 or the Police singing in their language. What I want to hear is *their* music, the roots music. The first thing I remember, going to Morocco, was the street musicians—the way they're subdividing the beat is *crazy*. It's kind of African, and it sort of reminds me a little bit of a Brazilian thing, but not exactly. It's still in time, but it's *weighted*. That's where the infinite comes in.

The infinite . . .

I happen to be one of those people who thinks time is infinite but also very scientific. You're in time or you're not in time, to me—I mean, everybody should at least be able to work with a metronome and then turn it off if you want. But what happens in time, in terms of *feel*, is that there's an infinite number of ways you can subdivide.

I can't help applying the same thought to pitch—blue notes have endless subdivisions and distortions of their own.

Right. When you're dealing with a non-pitched instrument, whether it's a fretless bass or the voice or anything, you're always kind of sliding into pitch, and how you slide—how you get from one note to another—is where you get the uniqueness of somebody.

That's where it gets crazy, right? I mean, there's "who we are," which is hard enough to quantify, but then that "person" carves a unique opinion into the relativity of time, the relativity of pitch, the relativity of everything. And then we call it a "song"?

I'm not a religious person at all—I'm not an atheist, either— but I've always thought that music is an example of—how can I put it?—"noncorporeal" energy. And I think it's so much easier, maybe, to think about things without a body or without physicality when you're blind. Especially if you've never seen. I don't know what anything looks like. I don't know what people look like. So, everything is abstracted to a different point. In the same way, everything is in your mind when you're dealing with something as ephemeral as music.

You've been called pop, jazz, singer-songwriter, blues, "world music," but none of them fit you. How do you deal with that?

I completely accept it now. I've stopped caring about what the industry thinks of me. You know, when you're in the middle of it and you're on a label and you're meeting people every day, you start getting caught up in that world of "How is this going to fit my brand" and all that crap. I have no interest in that anymore. I just don't care. I write what I write.

Eleven

RHYME AND REPETITION

In 2010, Stephen Sondheim, one of the most celebrated names in musical theater, wrote his memoir, *Finishing the Hat: Collected Lyrics (1954–1981) with Attendant Comments, Principles, Heresies, Grudges, Whines and Anecdotes*. In it, he stages an impassioned and brilliant defense of perfection in rhyme. By "perfection," he means rhyme should be exact (*home/roam*) and nothing less (*home/alone* does not cut it). Sondheim blames a lot of the smeared rhymes in pop music on laziness or some pretension that "spontaneity" retains energy that "song craft" hammers the life out of. He writes, "There is something about the conscious use of form in any art that says to the customer, 'This is worth saying.'" I love his use of the word "customer," and I personally love the idea of super-serving one—it gives them the feeling they're flying in business class.

Rhyme also lands thoughts on a repeated sound, and our recognition of that pattern gives a sense of "rightness" that I think we'd all love to bottle up and spray all over everything—as if order in art will order our world, make our beds, flip the perfect pancake.

Rhyme is a tool of persuasion, and it's not just for songwriters, or even for art. Johnnie Cochran, defense attorney for O. J. Simpson in a murder case that captivated the nation, dropped a rhyme bomb about a bloody glove that was found on the scene: "If it doesn't fit, you must acquit." It was a testament to the power of rhyme, if not of law. Of course, if it were *actually* true, a trial that lasted months would have taken about thirty-five seconds. "Okay, O.J., just try the gloves on, and let's be done with this." Prosecutors never countered in rhyme ("Bruno Magli shoes/the smoking gun of clues" or something), and I'm not saying they should have. I *am* saying that rhyme has internal power that extends beyond the words being rhymed. The ability to access the repetition the brain likes is one of rhyme's defining powers. Using it can deepen an argument, making the "right" sound "right-er." If that's what we're looking to do in our songs, rhyme is one way of getting it done.

There's a counterargument that the maintenance of order in art is, by nature, the maintenance of the roots of that order. It asks, *Who sets the standards of beauty, and in which ways are we complicit in upholding those standards? Is the adherence to the "rules" of art an adherence to a tradition of oppression, patriarchy, class, and/or privilege? What would our art, unmediated by form, be? If a song isn't rhyming, is it* really *out of laziness?*

Telling You How to Rhyme Is Like Telling You How to Live

I made this mistake in my very first class when I suggested a rhyme to a student that landed in a more "finished" kind of way. From the back of the room, someone chimed in, "Frank Ocean doesn't do that, and I *love* his stuff."

A little snark hasn't stopped me from calling out lines and phrases that I know a student can beat, but we can't deny that the radio, the charts, and maybe that playlist you made earlier in this book are awash in rhyme that is, well, not rhyme. I'm not saying it doesn't *work*, but I am saying that it doesn't rhyme, by the definition of the word "rhyme."

There's an aphorism known as Hanlon's razor: "Never attribute to malice that which is adequately explained by *neglect*." (I've heard it stated other ways, but this is the most empathetic.) In class, when a song uses non-rhymes, slant rhymes, singers who rhyme "book" with "love" by torturing the vowel and burying the consonant at the end, I'll check in with it. Maybe they didn't notice. Maybe they just ran out of time and had to get something in before class. Maybe they think it works. Maybe it does.

But in recent years, some students have said to me that they *would* have rhymed a line, but the *fact that it rhymed* made the line seem contrived. Instead of the rhyme energizing the line, it *flattens* it because we knew it was coming. In *Working on a Song: The Lyrics of "Hadestown,"* Anaïs Mitchell puts it well: "The perfect end rhyme waves its arms and shouts, 'Look Ma, I made a rhyme!'" As great as the rhymed word is, its sonic predictability can drain some of its power. The puzzle's too easy (no dopamine). Now, when I see the rules being bent, broken, or abused in *intentionally subversive* ways, it crosses my mind that something more may be going on.

Instead of seeing if a line rhymes, maybe the more inclusive word is "lands." That's what we really want, right? A line that *lands* will give you that drop in the stomach or the crack of a punch line that can bury an ex, pull the floor out from under a thought, or send you flying. If you've played a lot live, especially in a solo setting—just you and your instrument against the world—you live and die by these lines. They set the audience up, which binds them together, which gets them to lean in, which turns them into fans.

If the brain likes to be right, *but not consistently*, then a strong case can be made for pulling our lyrics out of lockstep. Verses that don't rhyme set up the expectation of normal speech, but if they *do* rhyme, the listener gets the message that, as Sondheim put it, "this is worth saying."

Maybe that's the defining factor: *intent*. Intent doesn't necessarily rhyme, have rhythm, or make any sense whatsoever. But if the heart of the song dictates the form being used, it dictates the rhyme scheme, too.

Can we feel structure? Yes. Absolutely. So, in figuring out what structure to use, consider: How do you want your listener to feel? Do you want them to feel like they're in good hands? Or do you want them to meander through the song by giving long, unbalanced lines that rhyme sometimes (but maybe not) because that's the natural beauty of life? Is what *you* want also what the *song* wants? These are the questions being argued and answered in every choice we make, and as culture shifts, the argument shifts with it. Language is alive. Songs are a language.

Repetition

Here's a wound from early in my teaching career: After listening to a student's song in class, I recommended he repeat a phrase. He asked, "Why?" and before I could respond, a disgusted student hissed, "Because we're not in a music class . . . we're in a music *industry* class." I didn't sleep that night.

Song sections repeat, but why? When we rhyme, we repeat a sound, but why? Martin Luther King Jr. repeated the phrase, "I have a dream," but *why*?

Philosophers and writers—Plato, Kierkegaard, Nietzsche, Vico, Woolf, and McLuhan, to name a few—have agonized over the roots of repetition. They discuss past lives, time spirals, eternal returns, and the possibility that repetition doesn't even exist. All of which is fascinating, but if I'd answered my student's question—"Why repeat stuff?"—with, "Well, class, gather 'round. *Nietzsche once said . . . ,*" they'd have walked out. Music, like philosophy, is abstract, but it's also intensely physical—just hug a kick drum while someone is wailing on it—and dry philosophical explanations don't satisfy in that way. I wondered if a universal answer might come from the universe itself. So I asked an expert.

It's Space Time

I met Janna Levin at a grand opening party for a mutual friend's robot factory. She's a cosmologist, the Claire Tow Professor of Physics and Astronomy at Barnard College of Columbia University, a Guggenheim Fellow, chair and director of sciences at Pioneer Works, and author of *Black Hole Blues and Other Songs from Outer Space*, which tells the story of the fifty-year search for the sound of colliding black holes as they "slosh in space-time . . . like waves on an ocean."

Songwriters and astrophysicists have an affinity for repetition. It's frequently used as a tool in music, but for astronomers, there seems to be an assumption that repetition is indicative of intelligent life—or at least that the possibility can't be taken off the table.

Absolutely. One of the things SETI—the Search for Extra Terrestrial Intelligence—does is that they look for very regular mathematical signals because they assume that nature won't provide such a thing—nature's messy, and so nature can't do anything so regular. So if you find an incredibly regular signal, you're hoping that it was sent by somebody who controls their environment, you know, who made it go that way.

But sometimes we're wrong about that. Have you heard about pulsars? So: There are big stars that collapse and die, and they don't quite make black holes—they're not big enough—so they make a neutron star. And the neutron star is spinning, and it has a huge magnetic field, and it basically becomes a lighthouse. It literally has a beam of light, and as it spins, that beam sweeps past you, *not* irregularly—radio astronomers detected one, and it was *clock on*, man. Clock on! I don't remember if it was a millisecond or a second sort of timescale. But it was like, *boom, boom, boom,* so regular that they jokingly called them LGMs, which meant "little green men." And then over time, they realized this is a natural source. It's just a perfect clock. Over billions of years, it will not slow down. And it will not waver. And that can happen, that nature makes something that's so perfect.

What does it say about us that we're so intrigued by repeated information?

I am a big believer that we inherit mathematical structures because math made us. Evolution is guided by forces of nature—that's how we evolve—and those forces, not surprisingly, leave an imprint in the structure of our minds. What else is going to be left there, something magic, some magic *thing,* you know? So what do we have but the forces prescribed in our minds, which are certain structures, how the neurons connect? Of *course* they have to be mathematical. And in some larger, genetic sense of who our family was, who our parents were—our parents were the laws of physics. And in our minds, it's encoded there. And we're discovering the structure of our minds.

There are also communications within the animal kingdom, like birdcalls, that repeat. And the repetition corrects for errors. So, you know, if you didn't get it the first time, you get it the next time . . .

We want to be unique in language, but we also want to be repetitive enough that you recognize the words. I want to say those words to you over and over and over again, like with children. And then they acquire language. You need the repetition first to understand what the words mean, but then I want to be able to say something unique by assembling those words in a certain way.

That's a basic theory of songwriting—choruses that repeat and teach themselves to the listener . . .

Right. LIGO [the Laser Interferometer Gravitational-Wave Observatory that has recorded the sound of black holes colliding] has a real hard time detecting something that only bursts *once*. It has to *repeat* for it to be able to pull it out. In fact, one of the things we really hope from LIGO going forward is that it will hear something for long enough that it'll be able to hear repetitions—that's *exactly* what it's going to want to look for. And those repetitions will allow it to identify something.

That's what I'm talking about!

That's what science is about—reproducibility, experimentation, the fact that somebody else can do it and get the same answer. I was talking to someone from Oxford who said, "Look, this is a real experiment: In your mind, imagine a circle, divide it by the diameter. You have just derived the formula for pi. That is an experiment. And anybody can do the same experiment in their minds and get exactly the same answer." I consider that to be as tangible as anything. It might not mean that I physically, externally, took out a tape measure, right? But that is as real to me as if I had, and in some sense it's *more* real because my tape measure is imperfect, but in my mind, it's perfect. How is that not real? That's *real*.

So, repetition, whether from the same source or the same computation, makes something real.

I think a lot of people who are as inclined as I am toward abstraction struggle with "reality" because it's *less* real. "What do you mean that chair was blue? I think it's *persimmon-*colored." "I think it's *lavender*." Like, there's less reality in reality than there is in our minds. So it's quite comforting to know that if you're from Bangladesh, 200 years ago, and you did the same pi thought experiment, it's 3.14159 et cetera. There's a sense of connectedness that's very profound. *Very* profound. So I think if you think of repetition as an evolutionary trait, then it makes sense that we have it.

Twelve

WHO ARE YOUR COLLABORATORS?

When the Hit of the Summer wafts across the pool at a weekend barbecue, my friends who aren't in the music industry wag their hamburgers at me and say, "Mike, are you going to tell me it took twelve people . . . to write *that*?"

In a way, I'm glad people have become aware enough to even *ask* about how songs are written. This is not a fluke: writers and advocates have worked hard to raise awareness—both in public and on Capitol Hill—about how songwriters should be credited and compensated. I try to do my part by giving my irritated friends a recap of the process.

What I *want* to do—and I've never done this because I'm *trying to enjoy the barbecue*—is point at the burgers they're holding. I want to say that a "simple" song with many cowriters bothers them, but what *doesn't* bother them is that their burgers contain the meat of dozens, maybe even hundreds, of different cows. I want to say, "Are you going to tell me it took 100 cows . . . to make *that*?"

I realize that's hostile. And maybe hypocritical—I mean, I don't know how many cows is too many cows to eat at once. Do you? My friends probably don't know, either, but since they're such inquisitive types, I looked into it. The burgers, I mean.

Apparently, an average 100-cow burger begins its journey in massive feedlots in the Texas panhandle, where one-fifth of the U.S. beef supply originates. While awaiting slaughter, hundreds of thousands of cows produce millions of tons of manure, all of which dries in the Texas sun. Hooves and tractors then kick it up into dark fecal dust clouds the locals call "shog." (It's like fog, but with a *sh-*.)

Okay, so I won't go through the rest of what I learned about burgers, but eventually all of it, cows, shog, and so much more, winds up between the buns at the barbecue. But the multi-writer *songwriting* process is what bugs my friends?

Where Cowriters Come From

Our ability to work in teams defines us as a species. How did we figure out teamwork was a good idea? The way I understand it—and this is explained well in Yuval Noah Harari's book *Sapiens*—is that millions of years ago, we got hit with a double shot of evolution: We got large heads and the ability to walk upright. Walking freed up our hands for foraging and tool use, and nature selected for narrower hips to make our bodies more efficient. Our aching skeletons still haven't recovered, but, more important, many narrower-hipped women died in childbirth. Nature selected for shorter pregnancies, and women who gave birth earlier to smaller offspring did better; as a result, humans are basically born premature, relative to other species. We know this because human babies, cute as they are, are useless for a long time. No offense to babies, but other species have kids who are pretty much up and running moments after arrival.

These helpless human babies required care, and their parents needed food and help—the advancement of the species depended on it. So, they began banding together into mutually beneficial collectives, and in order to keep the band together, they sharpened their social and political skills. In short: In order to survive, they *collaborated*, and we've been doing it ever since.

The shadow side to all this evolution is that it's happened too quickly for our brains to internalize. Remember, we were not the apex predators we are now; without developed tools and a social network, we were snacks for tigers. And contained somewhere in our forward-evolving brains is millions of years' worth of reminders that we're slow runners, bad climbers, inept swimmers—unimposing, nonvenomous, flightless, and neurotic for good reason. Even now, we remain scared of our own shadows and wary that everyone's out to get, as in *eat*, us. To collaborate fearlessly, there's a lot that needs to be unlearned and replaced with that skittish word: trust.

Yes, and . . .

In *Creative Quest*, drummer/author/polymath Questlove describes a "high-flow creativity" tool that he absorbed from his years as bandleader of *The Tonight Show*, hosted by comedian Jimmy Fallon. It's an improv-comedy tool known as "Yes, and . . . ," or the act of taking whatever a scene partner gives you and spinning it forward into something neither of you would have come up with on your own. When "Yes, and . . ." is in the room, the room becomes, in Quest's words, a "collaborative and generous environment."

I spoke with Phil LaMarr, an actor and comedian with a long and distinguished career: You might know him as Marvin, the guy who got his head blown off in *Pulp Fiction*, or as an original featured cast member on *Mad TV*. He has supplied the voices of Hermes Conrad in *Futurama*, Green Lantern in *Justice League*, various characters in *The Lion King* and *Incredibles 2*, and in the video games *Final Fantasy*, *Mortal Kombat*, *Kingdom Hearts*, *Metal Gear*, and okay, I'll stop. *But* he has also taught improv comedy at the Groundlings, the famous L.A.-based school with alums including Jimmy Fallon, who most likely has explored the "Yes, and . . ." concept that Questlove picked up.

Where did you first encounter "Yes, and . . ."?

Sophomore year at college—a buddy of mine spent the summer taking improv classes in Chicago and said, "Hey, why don't we start an improv group?" And so he got us all together, and one of the things he handed us was this sort of improv Bible, which was a list of quotations and ideas. Some of them are taken from this old book in the seventies by Keith Johnstone called *Impro*, and some are things that were just said over and over at Second City for years: "Wear your characters as lightly as you wear a top hat; always play at the top of your intelligence . . ." But the core one—the very first one on that list—was "Yes, and . . ." The idea is that whatever your scene partner offers, whether it's a word, an emotion, a gesture—you listen to it, you take it in, you *accept* it—"*Yes*"—and then you build on it. It's not enough to just agree; you have to take it and add to it. It really is a philosophical thing: The only way for you to create onstage spontaneously is by building and collaboration.

Where do you pull from in order to build on an idea?

Anywhere. Because as long as you trust that your partner will agree, whatever you say can't be wrong. It's different than theater, because theater is about *conflict*—war is much more fun to watch than peace. But conflict works when it's *constructed*, because the writer will determine what the resolution of the conflict is. In improv, when you're creating, you can't have conflict because it just leads to dead ends. "Hey, I had this idea . . ." "*No.*"

Songwriting sessions share some of the DNA you're describing. A central concept might be agreed upon, but the improv element is definitely there.

With improv, usually you'll get a suggestion from the audience, or you'll have some sort of starting point, and all of us can interpret anything differently. But the first person to *declare* their interpretation is what you take and build on. It doesn't mean theirs is necessarily the best, but it's what you're given.

See, my question there, and it's obvious I'm not an improv person for asking it, but: What happens when you're given something that sucks?

Well, this is the thing: As long as you're moving forward, you can always get to a better place.

So, no idea sucks when you're an improv person.

Right. The key to "Yes, and . . ." is that it *shuts off* our judgment. You don't have *time* to judge. And it's something I always used to tell my students at the Groundlings: Coming up with ideas fast is not hard. Our brains are supercomputers. You can come up with any number of responses to anything. The hard part is deciding *which one*. And once you have that judge in your head like, "What is the *best* thing I can do right now in front of this audience?" you're crippling yourself. Or someone will say something—and this is where the ego can be problematic—and it's like, "Why do I have to take *their* idea just because they said it first?" The truth is, if you let your ego get in the way, your idea is not going to be good because it's not going to connect to the one that came before, and all of a sudden your great idea is now random and out of place and doesn't track . . . and you've broken the scene.

Can you practice getting the ego out of the way?

One of the things we focus on is "listening" as opposed to "planning." And one of the other tenets after "Yes, and . . ." about four or five down is, "Make your partner look good." Because then, if somebody gives you something that sucks, it's like, "Okay.

How do I save them?" And then you toss them something that allows them to do something better. You have to "Yes, and . . ." in the direction you have been "Yes, and . . ."-ed. The person who builds on what they're given will find themselves going someplace that nobody expected. And that's always going to be better than any one piece someone has to offer.

Doing that live sounds pretty nerve-wracking.

I've known great actors who were deathly afraid of improv. Like they say: The actor's nightmare is that you're onstage under the lights and you have *no idea what the play is.* For an improviser, that's a Tuesday.

Credit Where It's Due

Back to the barbecue: Let's talk about what we see in the credits and what we don't.

Division of Labor

In a 2020 interview with Music Ally, Spotify CEO Daniel Ek put his vision of the future bluntly: "You can't record music once every three to four years and think that's going to be enough." His comments drew fire from creators—*Who made you the boss of songwriting?*— but even so, many music makers have taken cues from other industries and moved to a mass-production model.

Some people in the pop world focus solely on beat making, which is exactly what it sounds like: making beats, or tracks, that can form the bed of a song. There are "topliners," who, as we've discussed earlier, write melody lines and lyrics on "top" of those tracks. And there are producers who have enough of a hand in the shaping of a song to deserve—or demand—credit as songwriters. The names add up quickly, and the speed of output increases. Is the quality affected? Some would argue it *improves* because it prevents overthinking and the tyranny of a single perspective—the more people contribute, the less specific and more *universal* the song becomes. Some would argue the quality declines as an endless glut of songs roll off a conveyor belt. Some just like to argue.

Recommendation for you: Don't argue. Write songs.

Sampling and Interpolating

If you're on a songwriting team and you've written a song that samples or borrows heavily from *another* songwriting team, *credit must be given*. Students ask me all the time, "Can I just use this little teeny, tiny piece from Miles Davis's *Kind of Blue* and maybe change the key and run it through a baby monitor so it sounds a little different?" No. No, you can't. A thousand times: No. Lawyers will confiscate your entire life. There are so many examples of this kind of bad judgment that I won't even bother naming one because by the time you read this paragraph, there will be another. And seriously, you can't figure out how to re-create something close or even create something better? I bet you can.

When samples are cleared legally, interesting groupings show up in the credits: Among the ten writers and three producers on Ariana Grande's 2019 hit "7 Rings" are Richard Rodgers and Oscar Hammerstein II. They are the duo behind "My Favorite Things," from 1959's *The Sound of Music*, which forms a great deal of "7 Rings." This means that they cowrote a hit despite both being dead for decades. Likewise, Haim's "Summer Girl," released in 2019, was influenced strongly enough by Lou Reed's 1972 classic "Walk on the Wild Side" that he is credited as one of the six writers on the song despite having died in 2013. If the dead are still cutting deals and making money, I think you have to ask: How dead are they?

Revision

All art is subject to rounds of revision, and in pop music, the writers or producers who are brought in to "punch up" a verse or rework a post-chorus get added to the credits. These writers may never meet. Some guests I've had in class have told me *they* didn't even know who worked on a song until they read the credits on release day. That's also when they find out that the percentage they thought they were going to get on the song has decreased. The consolation is that the song may have improved, and their share might have gotten more valuable. (In the words of songwriter Sarah Solovay, "I'd rather have 50 percent of a watermelon than 100 percent of a grape.")

Several writers have come into my class and advised to be firm in representing your contributions (especially if you're a woman) but ultimately not to wreck relationships over relatively small differences in percentage. Getting less than you think you deserve can suck, but far worse is to be excommunicated from the clannish songwriting teams that will be cranking out many more songs in the future. It takes a little political restraint and maybe some breathing exercises.

Avoiding a Lawsuit

Producer Benny Blanco came to my class and told this story: He'd been working on a song titled "Me and My Broken Heart" with pop band Rixton, and it became apparent that it sounded a *lot* like the Rob Thomas song "Lonely No More." Instead of abandoning the song or risking a court date, they simply called Rob up, explained the situation, and offered to cut him into the songwriting credit. Rob agreed. Done and done.

Ironically, Rob Thomas came to my class on a separate occasion and explained the music business expression, "Where there's a hit, there's a writ." In other words, if your song pops, chances are someone may come out of the woodwork with a "writ," which is a formal term for a legal document, like the one you'd get for copyright infringement.

Whether you're in the right or not, it's a headache. Artistically, it can cast shade on your art. Financially, if there's a pending legal case, performing rights organizations that collect royalties (ASCAP, BMI, SESAC, and so on) will hold those royalties in escrow, and *no one gets paid* until the situation is resolved. This can mean millions of dollars, held for many years.

The courts have shown that relief is not ensured. Copyright is a fluid topic, and juries determine "infringement" based on legal precedent, persuasive lawyers, expert witnesses, and their own best judgment. This means you can be completely in the right and still lose. This is *not* legal advice, but there's a saying in the financial world: "Bulls make money. Bears make money. Pigs get slaughtered." If you need to cut someone in, the end result might be that you receive a smaller piece of the pie, but at least you can *reach* the pie.

Don't be a pig.

Muscle

If a popular artist wants to record your track, they may get a piece of the writing credit, even if they've done nothing. Well, not *nothing*, exactly. They bring juice—their name—to the table, and that gives a song a much better shot than if someone unknown releases it. You might say "bringing juice" is not a songwriting technique, and you'll get no argument from me. I'm just telling you what happens.

But it doesn't have to, and here's a quick story about the power of saying "no." In 1974, after several years as a mainstay on *The Porter Wagoner Show*, Dolly Parton, prolific writer and all-around shining light, decided it was time to pursue her solo career. Reflecting on her split from the show, she wrote "I Will Always Love You" and brought

Porter to tears. The song was released on her 1974 album *Jolene* and hit #1 on the country charts.

Elvis Presley fell in love with it and wanted to record his own version. Dolly, of course, was thrilled—until Elvis's manager, Colonel Tom Parker, called. In an interview with CMT, she remembers, "[Parker] said, 'Now, you know we have a rule that Elvis don't record anything that we don't take half the publishing.'" The song had already been published and had already been a hit, but that didn't seem to factor into the "negotiation"/demand. It was Elvis, after all. But Dolly didn't blink. "I said 'I'm sorry' and I cried all night . . . and I just didn't do it, and they just didn't do it. But I always wondered what it would sound like. I know he'd kill it. Don't you?" Elvis never recorded "I Will Always Love You," but in 1992, Whitney Houston did, and it went on to be one of the best-selling singles of all time. Dolly: "When Whitney's [version] came out, I made enough money to buy Graceland."

What's *Not* in the Credits

The more you lay out the reasons why songwriting credits have lengthened, the more that Hit of the Summer starts to resemble that multi-cow shog-burger at the barbecue.

But there are more abstract forces that shape a song as much—or maybe even more—than cowriter(s). We play "Yes, and . . ." with them, and they're never late for the session because they never leave.

Here are some—let's call them "shadow collaborators." I've also tossed in some prompts to help you get to know them better.

Silence

Our first collaboration is with whatever preceded the collaboration. For each sound we contribute, silence "Yes, and"s us with the possibility of electrically charged pauses, the crest of an arrangement before the beat drops, the time-bending terror of a soundtrack that cuts out as the camera pans to the babysitter, who's slowly turning the closet doorknob, and . . . *aaannnnd* . . .

Journal prompt: List some memorable silences—in songs, in the weather, in sex, in thought. Describe that silence's surroundings and see if there's something there you can collaborate with.

Time

We're dropped into an ongoing historical narrative, and there may be wars, or peace, or a pandemic, or the Renaissance . . . we get no say. It's the present, it's the 1950s, it's 1122, it's 2250, like a needle skipping on vinyl. It's Paris, it's Bogotá, it's Detroit. As frustrated parents say to frustrated toddlers, *You get what you get, and you don't get upset.* We work with what we get.

Journal prompt: What time are you writing in? Because it's not always now. And where? Because it's not always here. Give yourself a time machine, travel to the time and place you want to collaborate with, and take notes. Get the bizarre details but also the recognizable human responses to them. Also: Your time machine is able to uncouple place and time, so they don't need to be concurrent—you can be, say, an ancient Egyptian goddess in the International Space Station. Wherever you end up, consider the space and time you once had, you now *have*, you still have *left*.

Business Pressure, aka Time II

Songwriter Sammy Cahn was asked which came first for him— music or lyrics. He answered, "The phone call."

Business can be urgent, demanding, and inspiring, especially when rent is due. The "muse," on the other hand, is basically like a marginally interested house cat that wanders in and out of our lives. When it's around, that's nice, but when it's not, there's no waiting around for it to show up. If the phone call says we need a 6/8 acoustic indie track or an inspirational topline for "a Katy Perry–type artist" by end of day, then you've just met your collaborator, cat be damned.

Journal prompt: Write an inspirational 6/8 acoustic-based indie-pop song for a Katy Perry–type artist by end of day. I'm not kidding. End of day.

Money

Years ago, I cut out a crudely drawn, single-paneled cartoon from a magazine—I forget which—and stuck it onto a corkboard over my desk. In it, a shaggy-looking artist type is standing between a canvas and a clean-cut businessman. He's holding a paintbrush in one hand while stretching the other out, palm up, toward the businessman. On the canvas is an exact replica of the businessman's face and, in bold letters beneath him, the words

> F U C K I N G
> A S S H O

The speech bubble above the artist reads, "Can I have a grant so I can finish my art?"

Money often dictates the size and scope and even the content of the work. And if that's true, then who steers the course of art history—the artists or their financial backers? Conversely, some of us want to write commercial pop music because it "pays," but what if it didn't? If we knew no funding was possible, what would we write? Would we even bother writing?

Journal prompt: David Lee Roth, lead singer of Van Halen, said, "Money can't buy you happiness, but it can buy you a yacht big enough to pull up right alongside it." Is that true? Bank robber Willie Sutton was asked why he robbed banks. He responded, "Because that's where the money is." Is *that* true? Don't forget: Van Halen broke up, and Willie spent a lot of time in jail.

Venue

Jennifer Rowley, soprano for the Metropolitan Opera, among others, can soar over an orchestra and fill Lincoln Center; Norah Jones can sound like she's one pillow over, whispering in your ear. These are collaborative choices based on sensitivity to the venue. How important is it? This important: When I was a kid, my grandmother, the opera singer, would occasionally tuck me in at night, kiss me on the forehead, and ask if I'd like to hear a lullaby. Before I could dive under the blankets, she'd launch into the final scene from Puccini's *Tosca* at window-shattering volumes.

Journal prompt: Which venue collaborates most effectively with your songwriting? Is it the stretched, vaulted stonework of St. Peter's Basilica? A low-ceilinged basement dive? A Jeep with sub-basses that require an extra car battery? An outdoor festival with a million-dollar sound system? A king-sized waterbed with zebra-striped sheets? Describe it in detail and *collaborate with it.*

Politics

We live within a system. The system is basically a fiction. It's written on paper, and the writers are dead. We honor the paper because we believe, or say we believe, in what the paper says. Then we fight about what the paper says. We believe people have inalienable rights and that we are created equal. Except that, when the paper was written, it wasn't true. Is it now? And where does that leave us? And what about the people who don't believe in our paper?

The characters that move through our work act in relation to those beliefs, tensions, and contradictions. They advocate for greater or lesser adherence. Some characters break the law justifiably in order to bring inequity into relief. I am referring, of course, to *Les Misérables*. Kidding, but not really. There are calls for revolution even in art that people get dressed up for and pay a lot to see.

Journal prompt: Do you want your politics to appear in your music? Do they already? Which politician, living or dead, would you like to write the campaign music for? What values would you stress or imply in that music? Tall order, but: What do you believe in?

Unlived Lives

Carl Jung wrote, "Nothing has a stronger influence psychologically on their environment and especially on their children than the unlived life of the parent." An "unlived life" is an alternate path that a parent or partner—or you—didn't choose, for whatever reason. Since what might have happened is unknown, an unlived life is easily mythologized, and it's an eager receptacle for regret and "should haves" (Bottom Right Quadrant: *I do not trust you/you are trustworthy*). Unlived lives become collaborators—they can be motivating or frustrating, often both.

People will foist these unlived lives onto others who appear to be living them, and it feels like being handed a dead body. "Dude! It's so cool that you're doing [whatever it is *they* want to be doing]. You're my hero! (I'm stuck!)" This happens to artists a lot, and when it happens to me, I know they're not really talking to me; I'm just a mirror that's too polite to walk away.

Unlived lives also look to commiserate with other unlived lives, but of course it doesn't help. Example: Despite my mediocre typing speed, I got a job working the graveyard shift in a typing pool at a fancy New York law firm. My friend gave me the gig before going off to Tokyo Disneyland to be Diamond Jim in the *Diamond Horseshoe Revue*. I was his insurance: if D-land didn't work out, I'd have to give the job back.

I sat next to a woman who was studying to be a gemologist and remember typing up patent applications for a sheik who'd come up with a harness-and-pulley system that would allow one to have sex while suffering with a bad back. There was another one for a revolutionary mattress with a pullout drawer for automatic weapons. Each application contained illustrations, charts, and graphs. These were design secrets that needed legal protection.

Around two or three in the morning, the lawyers would emerge for coffee and maybe a shower before getting into a spare suit. We'd stand in the cramped kitchen area, stretching our legs and drinking harsh coffee from company cups, and talk about where we'd all rather be.

There's only one way to unlive an unlived life: *Live.*

Journal prompt: Which unlived lives can you recognize around you? Inside you? Inside your loved ones?

Are you empathetic to them? Angry at them?

Do you mourn them?

Or do you live them for someone else's benefit?

Does it help those people?

Does it help you?

Spend some time with this one. It's a prolific collaborator.

The Bucket

Genre is a method of file management. It's a kind of bucket that catches related content. You might think of yourself as perfect for one bucket, to the exclusion of others. You may have adapted to the surrealism of streaming music's utility-based playlists; you see your-self as "Morning Coffeehouse" but probably not "Evening Coffee-house." Where there was no discernable difference before, now there is because, well, somebody invented a new bucket.

Buckets serve the consumer, and consumers love that, so they fill the "demand" side. As a creator on the "supply" side, you know that placement in the right bucket means you go from 750 streams to 500,000 overnight. So what do you do? *You write for the bucket.* The bucket is now your collaborator.

Journal prompt: Be your own damn bucket, and fill it. This is my bias, of course, and a lot of people don't buy it. I know people who make up fake bands and write real songs for them and then shoot at song buckets all day, like it's an arcade game. You could do that, and you might enjoy it. I'd just suggest that one of those fake bands be real.

Radio and Streaming

Lee Dannay is head of A&R at Thirty Tigers, a Nashville-based enter-tainment company that works with artists ranging from Jason Isbell and the 400 Unit to Lupe Fiasco. I asked her the barbecue-ruining question.

Why are there so many writers in the credits of a song?

I don't know that there's one succinct answer because every collaboration has its own intention. If you're signed to a major label, radio and streaming is paramount, so creative decisions get made with an eye toward what's going to work there.

Radio will say, "We need songs that will work on these sta-tions, in these formats, and on these platforms. How do we get them?" The label's answer started with, "Artists should work with X producer," and then the producers started being a little bit more involved in the writing process. It's a little chicken-and-egg: Did radio spark the need for cowriting, or did cowriting drive major labels' hope to spark a radio hit? My feeling is that labels have been more traditionally reactive to what works at radio, so, as radio has become very format driven, it sort of throws the issue back to the majors.

That's a big rabbit hole we just went down, by the way.

Let's keep going. What do you make of working by committee and focus group in this context?

I think the "A&R by committee" perspective has been born out of fear of not getting on radio. When I say "born out of fear," it's like everyone's afraid to be wrong or afraid to not have a hit, so you hedge your bets by working with people who are proven hit makers, whether that's a producer or a songwriter or both—the "writer/producer." The thought is, the more talented people you put in a room, the more you're going to get the best song—or the hit. I don't know that I *agree* with that, but I think that's one thought process on why so many people go into a room.

But there are other people who have other processes. There are A&Rs who work out of studios where they have people coming in and out all day throwing down different ideas, and then the overall producer—maybe with an A&R person—will cut and paste all those ideas together—"Oh, here's a great bridge," "Here's a great melodic change," or "Here's a great lyric hook"—and then somebody makes this Frankenstonian work of art, you know?

It's almost like A&R-ing a baseball team, right? You sign position players.

That's very true, and there's definitely as many people on a song as there are out on the field on any given day. And sometimes it's really great—that's not negative, it's just one way of doing things. And I think it's always done with the best of intentions. I don't think that any A&R person or publishing executive is entering into those collaborative efforts to water down the vision. You can look at pop music and be optimistic and see so many great things. You can also be really cynical because it's format driven and often made by committee. But then magic happens—and you get this great song.

How to Split the Invisible Pie

Cowriting and splits: These will break up a band because in truth there is no way to quantify collaboration objectively. I think the best we can do is come to an equitable agreement. If you're new to cowriting, here's a strong starting point: "equal splits." This means, if there are two people in the room, split songwriting credit 50/50. Don't get into who did what and how many bars one writer added or whatever. This means that, yes, classics like *The Best of Simon and Garfunkel* could just as well have been named *The Best of Simon, featuring Garfunkel Basically Being Handed Sheet Music*. But then, who's to say?

Here are some examples of how to look at splits.

Do the (Song) Math

Madison Emiko Love (the writer who keeps her journals in a safe) has been in pop music's biggest rooms and talked with me about how splits are calculated.

How do you split songwriting credit?

Every song has its own story. Some days, I'll write a song with a producer on guitar, just two people, and we split 50/50. If you start together in the room with two people or four people—everyone splits equal. That's what I believe. But sometimes you'll go into a session with a producer who has a track already made, and they take 50 percent off the top. Therefore, due to "song math"—which is something that someone should write a whole book on so that someone can follow it—there's only 50 percent left to split with the writers and the artists. But the rules seem to change a lot.

It becomes a matter of negotiating.

It can get messy. When there's a single with a big artist at stake, sometimes writers will stretch the truth and play a little dirty to get as much publishing as they can. Usually the publishers will work it out, with the ultimate goal being for everyone to just be fair and honest.

You've spoken about coming up and being a woman . . .

Yes. Female songwriters are still very much the minority. But also being a woman can be beneficial. A lot of female artists want women in the room to write with them, and, surprisingly, a lot of male artists want that as well so they get a female perspective.

I'm lucky. Most artists I work with treat writers with a great deal of respect. I worked on Lady Gaga's album [2020's *Chromatica*]. I wrote an idea with her producer. She ended up working on it without me and rewrote the whole song, blah, blah, blah. Then when it came down to [songwriting] splits, you know what she gave me? Equal splits. Because she's classy. Camila Cabello does that, too. She always gives equal splits, even if it's a concept she brings in.

How do you choose who to write with?

I have my "good" list and a "no" list that my publisher keeps track of. The "no" list has a little high-heel emoji on it—meaning, "No,

I'm putting my foot down, I will never work with those people ever again."

Without getting into specifics or anything, what would cause you to put your foot down on a cowriter?

Well, I don't like it when someone shows up very late to a session. It makes me feel like they don't value my time. Another example is that I don't appreciate it when anyone is smoking in the room. One time, I asked politely if they could smoke *outside*. They replied, "What will happen to you? Are you gonna *die*?" I said, "No, I am going to leave." So I grabbed my journal and walked out.

Family First

Shane McAnally began gigging at 12, appeared on the TV talent show *Star Search* at 14, and is now a Nashville legend. In 2014, he received the best country album Grammy for his work on Kacey Musgraves's debut, *Same Trailer Different Park*, and the best country song Grammy for cowriting her hit "Merry Go 'Round." (They won again in 2019 for "Space Cowboy.") He was named Songwriter of the Year by the Academy of Country Music and has gone on to write career-defining songs with Keith Urban, Kenny Chesney, Thomas Rhett, Kelly Clarkson, Sam Hunt, and Miranda Lambert, to name a few. In 2019, NBC premiered *Songland*, a song-based reality show featuring Shane as one of the on-air producers/mentors, and in 2020, he was named a Country Power Player by *Billboard* magazine.

How do you split songwriting credit?

Evenly. And I feel like that tends to be more of a Nashville way of doing things because we do tend to write with the same people a lot. And I think our thought is that maybe today you did ten percent of the work, but another day I may not be able to carry my weight. There's been very few instances where the splits have been different, but it has been because we weren't all in the same room. If we're all in the room, I have never had a case where I give someone less or was asked to give less. We let the chips fall where they do.

How do you get a cowrite started?

I have, at any given moment, hundreds of voice memos in my phone. A lot of times, I'll get things in the middle of the night, and it's almost like a message that doesn't seem to have any regard for what's going on around me. It feels cosmic—divine—when these ideas come. And because of the art of collaboration and bringing other people into songs, most of the things I start do not land where I think they're going to. Like, if I go into a room and I say, "This is what I was feeling, and what I have to be vulnerable and say," a lot of times I'm met with blank stares. That means that's just not the day for it. But there are also times where someone goes, "Oh my God, I was just watching something that reminds me of . . . ," and that usually means it was meant to be written, you know?

For a long time, I was sort of tricked by words and the sound of words without needing that next level. But in the last few years, when my collaborators come in with what I call a "bumper sticker" line, which is a really great phrase or something, I'll love it but will ask, "Where's the *heart*, where's the *thread*, and why will this stay with me later?" That's a common way of starting for the crew I write with.

In the time that you've been working, have you noticed any changes in song form?

Yes, absolutely. We've always been so *verse, chorus, verse, chorus, bridge, chorus*—that's a pretty good baseline. What switched in the last ten years was the post-chorus situation—"Merry Go 'Round" is a good example of a "traditional" song that has a post that feels like a surprise. Essentially, what we were doing is moving the bridge to follow the choruses. And what would happen is we'd get to what I call a "kickout bridge," which is when the first word of the bridge matches the last word of the chorus and they just go seamlessly. I didn't make that up. It just became part of what I love to do.

Then you get into the pre-chorus—pop songs, especially now, are just so A-B-C-D. You have the verse; the melody needs to change halfway through the verse; you need to get into a pre-chorus, then a chorus; and then the post needs to blow up. *Very* recently, we're writing second verses that are completely different melodies than the first. I think it comes from the need for us as humans to be entertained constantly. It's a direct line from the phone in that you are swiping and scrolling, and in the second verse, if you're already super familiar with that melody from the first, you're kind of like, *Whatever*. And that's where we're at in the streaming world. The skip rate has become so important in commercial music. Dua Lipa songs are such case studies for me because I love the songs, and the verses feel like choruses. And then all of a sudden you're like, "Holy shit, there's *another* one coming." You just gotta make sure they hear the part that's going to keep them from skipping. It's about how to keep everyone entertained.

It's interesting you mentioned that you write with a "crew." What do you look for in a crew member?

Well, in the beginning, I feel like the crew had to be assembled before any of us had success because your crew definitely grows when you get success. There are people that I love and consider family that I wouldn't have met had I not had hits, but it's that initial tribe, that crew, that kind of grows like roots. In commercial writing in country music and popular music, I just can't stress enough that it isn't in writing with someone who has hits—it's in finding someone who is like-minded, who sees the world as you do and can do something possibly that you can't. It's really hard to teach people that because you think there's, like, this magic potion that somebody who's had hits has, but they don't. It's *you*. *You* have it. And probably the person that has hits has it *less* than you because it's very hard to change as music changes. The young writer, the writer who hasn't had hits, is the one who's ahead of it because the rest of us can't help but be who we are and have done what we've done, which means if we're writing the songs on the radio, we're already behind the next trend.

That has been the absolute most important thing I have done—to find a crew of people who you can do this with together. I'll always have that history with those people. And they'll also have *time* for you. You know, at the beginning of a career, you want to spend hours and hours and *hours* going over something or working on a demo in the middle of the night. You won't always get to do that. People's lives get bigger and change, and you have families and kids. I appreciate that I had that time with those people. And even if you don't become a huge songwriter, that's where the heart of this is. I mean, we're storytellers, and we gotta be honest with people, and who better to be honest with than people who know you?

Percentages of Percentages of Percentages of Percentages

Eva Grace Hendricks is the lead singer and cowriter of the power-pop outfit Charly Bliss, a band that has been on a slow and steady rise; 2017's *Guppy* was included in several Best of the Year lists, and their live show has delivered on the promise of their recordings.

Can you tell me how you split royalties in Charly Bliss?

Here's the thing: I'm in a band with my older brother and my best friends. We all do whatever work we need to do to make sure that everyone feels like the splits are an accurate representation of the work that we're doing.

A good split keeps the band together.

It does. It really does. And a Charly Bliss song isn't a Charly Bliss song until all of us leave our mark on it. So we've tried a lot of different iterations, and basically what we've come to is that, among the four of us, what we make on the publishing side is always equal, and then the songwriting side is where we represent the primary songwriters who really did the bulk of the songwriting work.

That's amazing—part of it is representative of the individual, and part of it is representative of the group.

Exactly. It sounds complicated, but the thing that really works about it is exactly that. There is a space wherein the work that we're all doing together—and the effect of the group working together—is being accurately represented, *but* there's also a place where we can just be completely honest about the bulk of the work being done. Sometimes, the full 50 percent of the songwriting side goes to one person, and that feels more honest. We used to think we had a hundred percent to play with, but really you don't, I guess is the point that I want to make. You really have percentages of percentages of percentages of percentages. [*Laughs*] And I think, as long as there's a place where you feel like you can say, "All of the writing that I did *and* the ownership I feel over the song is accurately represented here," boom, that feels great.

Rethinking Collaboration from the Ground Up

Speaking at New York University's Clive Davis Institute in 2020, Jack Stratton, leader of the funk-based band Vulfpeck, presented a definition of collaboration that breaks free of the industry's past practices and builds a new vision. This is an excerpt of his conversation with musician and professor Marc Plotkin:

> As you break out of college and get into the "music industry," you'll find there are these bizarre dynamics where people will get in tussles over "creative equity." And it gets really awkward, and people get cagey about contributing creatively if they're a musician. So, I wanted to preserve the college vibe, where everyone is an "equity partner"—every dollar of a recording's profit gets split equally with everyone who played on it. It all goes into one Excel spreadsheet. I do all the [royalty] administration for the group.
>
> So, take our first song, "Beastly." Four people played on it. I wrote it. (Bassist) Joe Dart's solo is what made it great. Say it gets a $10,000 sync in a Hulu show: five grand goes to the rights holder, and five grand goes to the master owner. Traditionally, *I* would get that five grand as the writer, and the record label would get the other five grand. [In Vulfpeck,] I take that ten grand, put it into the Excel spreadsheet, and each musician—there were four—gets 25 percent of that ten grand.
>
> We [also] collaborate with the greatest musicians in pop music history: James Gadson, Bernard Purdie, David T. Walker . . . I mean, David T. Walker is the guy on [the Jackson 5's] "I Want You Back," playing all the guitar licks, and he was reading a lead sheet with the bass line and chords. So he's a *writer* to me. But these cats were getting paid union scale—which was a good deal at the time, you know—but imagine having back-end [royalties] on a track like *that*. We've played with Clyde Stubblefield, James Brown's drummer, who doesn't have writing

[credit] on "Cold Sweat"! The fricking horn player does; he gets a check whenever [it's played]. . . . It's ridiculous. So, now they're all cowriters, and this is a full "first principles redesign" of what a "writer" is in the pop context.

Writers right now should be stoked about what we're doing. Historically, there have been people who've made their careers off the writing side—I don't think that's going to happen as much anymore. So, we're trying this thing, like, "What if Google started the music business today? What would it look like?" This is just my little experiment. No one's buying a yacht here. They all get paid like great software engineers, you know? Like Google employees but with a really cool job. And I enjoy it, you know? And everyone else enjoys it, too.

Final Thought

I did a little more research, and it turns out it doesn't matter how many cows are in a burger. Cow quantity doesn't make the burger more or less healthy (or ethical) than, say, many people pouncing on a single cow. In the same way, songwriter quantity doesn't make a song more or less undeniable or nontrivial. Some manufacturing processes are weirder than others, I guess.

So, anyway, that's why I don't get invited to many barbecues.

Interlude: Five Gems from the A&R Department

I met with a rep from a major label who (anonymously) offered me five pieces of advice to pass on to you.

1. Write to the Left

For artists: "The core of why people do A&R is that they want to find exciting artists that aren't represented in the marketplace, and they want to fight for them. So, there's more upside in discovering an artist that's onto something totally new than an artist who follows in another artist's footsteps."

For writers: "I'll have conversations with writers who'll say, *I have a perfect song for X.* And they'll send me a song, and it'll sound like something that was on X's album, or it'll sound like something X would sound good on, but they don't realize that I'm hearing the best writers in the world and *their* best song for X. And X doesn't need not-as-good versions of things X has already put out. An artist wants songs that have a lyric, or a sense of something that speaks to them—something subconscious that maybe even *they* weren't aware of. They have to think, 'Wow, that's an incredible story, or lyric, or narrative that I *identify* with. And I would never write this myself, and I *have to sing the song.*'"

2. The Best Hit Songs Don't Sound Like Pitch Songs

"It has to be an 'artist' song—something an artist would become a fan of because *they* would listen to it. You have to think about the artists—where are they in their life? What is inspiring them musically? What do they *care* about? Sometimes that's hard to do in a pitch situation if you don't know the artists, but maybe you can get as much information as you can and try to channel that in your writing."

3. Artists Don't Like Demos That Sound Like Them

"Writers will send a demo that sounds like the artist they're pitching the song to. *Artists don't like that.* I've worked with lots of artists with 'big' voices, and we would get all these songs with singers that would try to sound like them and it was just—it was *bad*. People would even try to do the inflections or signature things that the artists do. That's just . . . *no*. 'Oh man, X is gonna love this.' [*Laughs*] It's funny how some writers think. But those songs never got cut."

4. If It "Sounds Like a Hit," Beware

"When someone says, 'It sounds like a hit,' I actually get a little bit worried because that means that it's borrowing from something someone else has already done. That can be good, but I'm always cautious of that phrase. It's behind the curve."

5. Set the Bar Higher

"Writers will say they have incredible songs, but they 'just need the right person to hear them,' and that's why they haven't broken through yet. But the reality is that the songs are just probably not good enough. The writers haven't pushed themselves hard enough. They maybe haven't worked on their craft enough.

"I used to work with an A&R guy, and every now and then, when a song was sent to him, he'd ask the publisher or whoever, 'Is this as good as "Bridge Over Troubled Water"?' And the answer would be, 'Well, no.' And then he wouldn't want to hear it. I mean, that's kind of extreme, but writers have to think like that—like the bar is that high."

Thirteen

FACING DOWN THE FIRST DRAFT

You're journaling. You're singing into your phone. Somewhere in the soup of notes and ideas is a song, but damned if you can find it.

You're lost.

Well, you're not alone. Picture a family trip to a Target store. The youngest gets distracted by a toy just as the rest of the family turns into the laundry soap aisle, and by the time she looks up, they've disappeared. This kid is *lost*—arms flailing, heart pounding inside her tiny little chest, eyes scanning a Target-red sea of the unfamiliar. Now picture the family tween, bored of laundry soap and craning his neck for the video games section. Now picture a teen, actively hiding from her stupid family that's all, like, "Check it out honey, Tide has a new extra-woodsy scent, makes ya wonder how they do it!" Finally, picture the parents, feigning vague interest in laundry soap but mostly navigating the meaning of shopping, family, capitalism, mortality.

Same Target! Same family! Same life!

Who's lost?

Everyone.

Everyone is lost, all the time.

So, Then, What *Is* "Lost"?

When we're "lost," we are separated from what we think we know. What do we think we know? What we think we know is what we think we *already* know. Repeated information, like a recognizable landmark, gives comfort. We are existentially relieved whenever we open an egg carton and find—whattya know—eggs.

But song drafts are uncomfortable. They're unfinished maps to nowhere because we still have to create the destination they're supposedly leading us to. We're stripped of the landmarks of memory and deprived of a recognizable path forward. This causes anxiety. So much of songwriting is about anxiety management. *What happens next?*

GPS = Gotta Point Somewhere

The anxiety of being lost really shows up, I think, after the first draft has landed with a thud, as it so often does. If it's a map to the song's end, where is the "X" that says "You Are Here"?

Anxiety is the space between you and finished. By the way, I'm not disputing that, yeah, you might be screwed. But I am disputing the nature of the anxiety over being lost. *Are* you lost? I mean, really? Or are you just a little, you know, turned around?

A root cause of our anxiety is that when we're lost, we reach for two terrible navigation tools: (1) the past and (2) the future.

Bad Tool No. 1: Why the Past Sucks

Part of the reason high school yearbook pictures are horrifying is not because you look idiotic, but because that person is gone. The two versions—this you and . . . *that* you—make less and less sense to each other as time passes. *Who was that kid? What was he thinking?*

In the same way, institutions I've left behind will invite me back for a "reunion," but I wonder, with *what*? Everything's different, including me. Memory—or nostalgia, which is just memory + vodka—is replaced by name tags and eyes that dart from tag to face, back to tag in disbelief, then again to face, lost in a calculation of *What the hell happened?*

Anxiety arises when we use the past to gauge where we are at present, because it doesn't work. It *can't* work. Think of Greg Felt and the river: we're comparing ourselves against something that is not a yardstick. Think of Janna Levin and pi: the profound "reality" of a repeated answer will never arrive if the variables have changed.

The past recedes, and though it owes us nothing, we can't help but feel stranded by it. Where we came from has dissolved into a kind of fiction we keep alive in the stories we tell ourselves, and each other. But there's no going back.

My point: We often look to the past for guidance, but the past is not reliable. And just because you think you recognize it doesn't mean you do.

Bad Tool No. 2: Why the Future Sucks

Sing it with me:

> *The bear went over the mountain*
> *To see what he could see*
> *The bear went over the mountain*
> *And what do you think he saw?*
> *He saw another mountain*
> *So what do you think he did?*

So school bus. So classic.

The bear? That's us. Another mountain, another mountain, another mountain. The mountain? That's our expectations. The song is written as a never-ending circle, but it ends. Oh, the song ends, all right. How does the song finally end? *The bear dies.* It dies in the shadow of another mountain, another mountain, another mountain. Does it matter *how* the bear died? No. The bear is dead.

The bear, if it was looking for anything, does not find it. There's no talk of what's at the top, no inkling of elation upon summiting, not even a rolling count of mountains climbed. The bear lumbers toward a future that never arrives. It's the tragedy of modern life. *Unless* the bear was going over the mountain *because that's what it loves to do.* And if a life spent going over mountains is the bear's passion, is it ever wrong? Is it ever lost? I would suggest: It is eternally *found.* And it has killed death by stripping it of its relevance. The bear goes because it goes, mountain after mountain, song after song—forever expectant and contented at the same time.

Wait, So If the Past and Future Both Suck, What's Left?

What's left is *right now.* And cowriting with it is possible.

Jay Joyce works out of a big stone church in East Nashville and blurs the lines between writer, performer, and producer. Through his work with Eric Church, Declan McKenna, Miranda Lambert, Cage the Elephant, Brandy Clark, Fidlar, Emmylou Harris, Coheed and Cambria, Little Big Town, and many others, he makes a good case for ignoring "how it's been done" in order to get to "how to do it *right now.*"

What do you do to get the best work out of writers and artists?

I don't have a vocal booth. People come in, and they're like, "Where do you sing?" And I'm like, "Wherever you want." I don't have a control room, you know. I never did like that. We don't have to be, like, "Put your guitar down, come into the control room." I can go on about the way studios are designed. It's just stupid.

I try to get people to just wing it. Start throwing syllables into the mic. And I try to get people *physically* to be performing, you know? Like, a lot of songwriters or artists write as a songwriter and then perform it. But with the great ones, part of the performance *is* their writing. You know what I mean? The way they might breathe and shorten a word or need a double syllable here or there. To me, if they give in to their performance, then it's going to be a better *lyric*. You get that feel of, you know, the tenth night out on a tour, your muscles are working, your strings are a little nasty 'cause you've been sweating on them. You know what I'm talking about. You're loose. You're, like, even not warmed up but you're *in it*, you know? If you can get somebody in that place recording, then they're gonna go way beyond what they even thought they could do, you know? Like, let things just *happen*.

How do you help that along?

Geez, it's always different, man. But, I mean sometimes you just play a lot. That helps, or creating diversions and making it more difficult for them. Maybe don't have such a great headphone mix. I don't do separate headphones for players. They all have to play to the same mix. Hell, I'll map out accidents intentionally, you know? Tell the drummer to do one thing and the bass player to do another and then get it. And they'll never do that accident again. [*Laughs*] You know, just things that kind of force the person to not be so focused on what they're doing.

It's so hard to get these guys that want to be songwriters to think outside of the box. Nowadays, everybody's got a list of sonic references, like, "Let's make it sound like this Radiohead song." Well, [Thom Yorke] wrote a different melody and it's a different, you know, *song*. It's like, they don't understand that you can't just give it a Radiohead raincoat and that's it, you know? So you wind up with this sort of bad rendition, maybe, rather than, like, "Let's just head in that general area, but let me throw a bunch of paint on the canvas, we'll see where it drips," you know what I mean? Then you're bound to get into something more interesting. And it's not a failure. [*Laughs*]

You Have One Job

In *A Field Guide to Getting Lost*, writer, historian, and activist Rebecca Solnit describes the act of losing our bearings as a kind of diving board into the deep end of transformation:

> Love, wisdom, grace, inspiration—how do you go about finding these things that are in some ways about extending the boundaries of the self into unknown territory, about becoming someone else?

Being lost feels *subtractive*—our ingrained understanding is being stripped from us—but it's actually *additive*; a flood of new, raw experience pours in. Our world grows "larger than [our] understanding of it," and we improvise our way through it using not what we know but *who we are*. Which is all a fancy way of saying: *It's our job to be lost.*

Quick Review

Scary: The familiar falls away.
Awesome: The unfamiliar appears.
These are the same.

Avoid the Avoidance

Philosopher Alan Watts: "At every moment we are cautious, hesitant, and on the defensive. And all to no avail, for life thrusts us into the unknown willy-nilly, and resistance is as futile and exasperating as trying to swim against a roaring torrent."

Give in. Surrender to a new definition of "lost" as the gain of a wider world. What arrives is a state of constant, breathless change—and the new person who gets to navigate it.

Hopefully, you can see how this approach can benefit an emerging song. When everything's unfamiliar, we're tossed out of ruts. All the paint boxes are open, and all the colors are available. We can't really achieve that in totally familiar surroundings. The limits we assumed we knew have dissolved. We're set free.

In between eating sandwiches delivered to him by his mom, Henry David Thoreau made a habit of getting lost on walks in the woods. I love quoting a pro: "Not till we have lost the world, do we begin to find ourselves, and realize where we are and the infinite extent of our relations."

The Joke's on You

I think part of what Thoreau means is that we aren't found after being lost—we're changed by the experience of it. We never really return. We walk into the woods as one person and emerge as someone else. In this same way, every draft—and every song—changes us. This means that, in gathering the guts to get lost, we are found. The flux we observe around us? *It's us.*

What I've noticed in my students (and in myself) is that, after singles or EPs or albums are sent off into the world, we wake up conversant in some other way of being. Everything may look the same, but we're ringing out like wind chimes from a subtle shift in the weather.

"Hey," he said, half-asleep, "what were you before you met me?"

"I think I was drowning."

A pause.

"And what are you now?" he whispered, sinking.

I thought for a second. "Water."

—Ocean Vuong, *On Earth We're Briefly Gorgeous*

The Gripping Conclusion

In talking to songwriters, what I've noticed is that when you are in the flow of writing, revising, finishing, and repeating the process, over and over, life and work take on a new, relaxed rhythm, and you will occasionally get those miraculous songs that arrive, almost entirely finished, in a matter of minutes. It happens to a lot of writers, and it's a blessed moment when there is simply no resistance in the cable. A channel opens up to "now," time "stops," and the song arrives. How did it happen? You just showed up, and one day, it showed up, too. How can you repeat it? Just show up.

You've probably noticed that this applies to more than just songwriting. You're right, and it's because, to me, it's all connected. I think it's true that we're clueless and that any kind of honest work forms a mirror, and every time we have to face it, we come up with a thousand reasons to discount our own eyes. But if we can withstand the resistance and revise, that mirror gets clearer, the reflection less avoidable, and the resistance more resistible. Inevitably, there is a reckoning: *Someone you took to be you is replaced by someone else who squints back at you, equally confused.* Not always easy! Often surprising! Sometimes awful! But each time a little clearer, maybe truer, and, for that alone, more beautiful.

How You Do Anything Is How You Do Everything

There's a short essay by Emily Flake titled "I Was in Charge of the Deck Chairs on the Titanic, and They Absolutely Did Need Rearranging." The narrator, a spirit whose job was to keep those chairs arranged, knows that we all laugh about how pointless it sounds but that she stands by her work. She's proud that the ship went down "with the loveliest deck amenities imaginable" and argues that the dignity of a job well done is all the reward we get in this otherwise indifferent life. Yes, she was dragged to the bottom of the North Atlantic, and no one will ever know how those deck chairs looked, but it doesn't matter because *she* knows. Now honored with solos in the choir of angels, she makes a case for the act of care: "How you do anything is how you do everything."

I've seen this thought play out many times. Students who show up and are deeply engaged become successful—and not necessarily at songwriting. I end up writing them recommendations for law school or arts grants; I congratulate them on their medical degrees or teaching gigs or advocacy work, anything at all. They came to play ball; they just had to figure out which ball to play. Care is a transferable skill.

I feel it when I glue my kids' toys back together. Why do I do it? Why have I reattached the broken windshield of a model Jaguar XK-E three times now? I don't know. Love? Because I want to *do anything the way I do everything*? Because it's who I want to be in this universe regardless how little it cares? In the end, I just know I can't have my boy push a Jag with a broken windshield across the carpet. Pass the Gorilla Glue.

And so, flipping the thought back onto songwriting: I'm going to guess that how you write songs is how you live the rest of your life. Care is a mindset. "Lost" is a mindset. Fear is a mindset. Love is a mindset.

Question: *Are you going to live with dignity, or not?* Because it's almost certain that that's all we get here. Eventually, you might find that you're better suited for something else. But your effort will show that you care, and the care is the win.

I shoot for the win, and I'm writing it here so that maybe you'll shoot for it, too. That Jag windshield is going to break more times than I'm going to fix it. But that's not what fixing it is about.

In the same way, ultimately, it's not about the finished song. The real point of the writing *is the writing*. The point of revising is the revising. When we're lost in the act, watching the sidewalk materialize under our feet, even death is just another moment. Life—expectation, history, the past, the future—passes by in that Jaguar windshield just like everything else, just like another something.

I never want you to be worried about being lost. Never again! I want you to find comfort in it, and inspiration in it, and humor in it. I want you to visit it and be familiar with it, like it's a friend.

You've got your walking shoes. Your emerging first draft. It's an imperfect thing, but it's a *first draft*. The U.S. Constitution has amendments, for crying out loud. Your draft can, too.

Let go.

Get lost.

Fourteen

THE FIRST DRAFT

In the famous horror movie *The Shining*, all hell breaks loose when Wendy Torrance, the wife of dissembling writer Jack Torrance, glances over Jack's draft manuscript and sees that all he's written is the sentence, "All work and no play makes Jack a dull boy" in an endless array of shapes and patterns. She freaks out, the music goes bananas, and Jack—played in the film by Jack Nicholson—snaps.

But, here's the thing. Jack's manuscript *was a draft*. You don't judge drafts!

What a nightmare breach of privacy this would be if it were to happen to you.

Who among us has not toiled over the same line to find how to set it just right? Who among us can feel a sliver of sympathy for Jack Torrance, Writer? Who among us suspects we've got a little Jack in us? Without the axe, obviously.

I'm not blaming Wendy for looking—Jack was getting loose in the turns, for sure. And I'm not excusing axe murder. I'm just, well, actually, maybe I am a little. I just want to protect your early drafts. No one should judge them, and if they do and they find themselves running for their lives in a shrubbery maze in the middle of a blizzard some night, well then, next time maybe ask permission.

What Is a Draft?

A draft is a baby song. Not a metaphor. It's real, alive, soft, and weird. It's unsure of what it is, and it's looking to you for clues.

You could ball your fists and growl, "Why can't you walk, yet, dummy?! What good are you?!" But that's not how babies learn to walk. Here's a tip: *Don't yell at babies.* When you do, nothing is on display but your *own* limitations. Not theirs.

This is to say that I hope you accept whatever starting point your first draft implies and revise with as much joy and as little frustration as possible.

Some drafts are further along than others, but that's no indication of how they'll turn out. You just raise the guardrails, stick bumpers on the corners of the coffee table, and get to work. Congratulations. You're a song-parent now. It can be a tough slog. But wow, when Baby gets something right, even if it's aiming a spoon into its own little song-face, you just want to high-five the moon.

Disclaimers

If half my life is spent listening to drafts, the other half is spent being prepped on why the draft I'm about to hear isn't worth hearing.

What I hear *before* I hear the song is (1) the writer's relationship with it, and (2) the writer's relationship with themselves. This is excusable *if* you're in a safe space, among friends or people who are truly on your side. But it's a bad habit for someone who's going to spend a career presenting songs to publishers, band mates, audiences, A&Rs, and so on. My former students can probably all say it with me: *Disclaimers don't work.*

Couples Therapy for You and Your Song

"So, okay, before you hit Play, I just want to say that I hate this song."

"Just warning you: I was in a weird mood."

"I wrote this in like five minutes."

"I think the chorus sucks."

"I think the verses suck."

"The bridge is just kind of a 'placeholder.'"

"Just hit Play—I'm going to wait outside in the hall. Come get me when it's over."

These (real) examples are just the short ones. Some disclaimers last longer than the actual song.

Again: *Disclaimers don't work.* They don't absolve us from what we've created. They don't suddenly orphan our song babies; we *all know* who the parent is. But disclaimers are even more destructive than that: They take the imaginary hole we think we're in and make it real. And they do this right before the song is played. If we think something is wrong and we call it out, that thing doesn't correct itself. The chorus melody doesn't change. The tuning doesn't improve. The wrong notes don't make themselves right. The crooked is not made straight.

In fact, whatever we call attention to *magnifies* in importance. So, if I'm about to listen and you tell me that the high G on the piano sticks, I'll become distracted from the heart of the work, and instead of listening, I'll form an opinion on sticky piano keys. When the song ends, instead of being productive, I'll say things like, "Oh, I don't know. I kinda like the G sticking like that," or "I know a guy who can fix your piano." This puts us miles away from the song, from constructive criticism, and from *the second draft.*

But that's kind of the point of a disclaimer, isn't it? It's a self-conscious, last-ditch smoke screen intended to pull focus. The tragedy is that, now that we've been distracted, *we can't help,* and you didn't get constructive feedback. You got the number for a piano tuner. Who loses?

Disclaimers Are the Opening Act for the Song

Have you ever been an opening act? I have. It's an art form—you become the living embodiment of the question, *Does it improve upon silence?* Every night, your main job is to justify why you're standing between the audience and the thing they paid to see.

Now: Imagine being the opening act and telling the audience, "I just want to let you know: The headliner sucks. No, really! I can't believe you paid for this crap. Well, anyway, thanks for coming out tonight, hope my explanation of the idiot headliner you're about to sit through was helpful. Be charitable because, like I said, their show really does suck."

Now imagine the audience reaction.

Now imagine being the headliner backstage, listening to the opening act.

Now imagine the opening act and the headliner crossing paths on the way to the stage.

Now imagine that the headliner isn't a seasoned act at all: *It's a baby.*

Now the baby has to go on.

Who loses?

How to Be the Best Presenter of Your Own Song

1. **Take all your disclaimers, apologies, and fears, and scream them into your journal.** Then go back and read them because they were not intended for your listeners—they're intended for *you*. Tip: *Disclaimers are a to-do list disguised as a plea for leniency.* They instruct *you* on how to tweak your prototype. They are a catalog of the itches you still have left to scratch.

2. **Work toward the day when you can put a song on for someone and just be quiet.** If you feel too vulnerable to do that,
   protect yourself by having done the work. Preparation lets you
   share from a position of power and calm. Like a ninja, really.
   Don't ninjas always seem weirdly calm? What do they communicate, with all that calm, all that *stillness*, if not the years in
   the dojo that can, at any moment, manifest in a single two-fin-
   ger punch to your spleen? We want to cultivate some of that.
3. **I don't care—and neither does anyone else—if you wrote it
   in five minutes or ten years or if it took you ten years to get
   to those five minutes or anything.**

Just hit Play.
"So, okay, before you hit Play, I just want to say . . ."
Shh.
"Just warning you: I was in a weird mood."
Shh.
"The bridge is just kind of a . . ."
Shh.
"The high G on my piano . . ."
Shh.
Just hit Play.

Revising the First Draft

Revision separates the pros from the amateurs. If revision isn't your
thing, then I suggest you get into something more fatality-adjacent,
like bullfighting or maybe BASE-jumping. This way, if you do it
wrong the first time, you never have to bother getting better.

Is Revising "Cool"?

Cleaning up our fever dreams goes against everything that made the fever dream feverish to begin with. For this reason, revision feels custodial. It's not windblown and thrilling, the way it was pictured in the songwriting brochure in our minds.

Look: We're not the audience. The rush of the final product is not for us to have. Like magic, no one else is ever supposed to know how it's done or how hard it was.

Out here, we songwriters revise constantly. There's not a song on the charts that hasn't been worked over a thousand times. And we're not especially burdened: There's not an appliance in your kitchen that didn't go through umpteen rounds of development, either. Teams of engineers popped a lot of puncture-proof tires to make the four you ride on.

Or think of it this way: to make a baby, sometimes it takes a bunch of tries.

Revision is work only if you think it's work.

Why Revise?

For one, it's generous to the listener. We're asking for people's *time*, and we have a responsibility to fill it wisely. When we revise, we're telling listeners that we've been working with them in mind. It's an act of care.

It's also generous to yourself. You'll be closer to the song's center, which is to say, *your* center. Which is to say, *our* center. Isn't that part of what this is all about?

Trusted Filters

Remember when I said, "Reality is nothing but a collective hunch"? Well, by choosing our collectives, we influence that hunch. That means, by definition, we *actively bend reality* based on the people we hang out with. Cults are the extreme example of this, but a tight-knit group of friends or writers who will give you contructive feedback can forge a picture of reality just as easily. Will our reality change our songs? Absolutely. Choose your reality wisely.

Songwriters write in groups and cliques because they like the collective reality they've created. They feed it as much as they feed off of it. They're open to ideas and people who can deepen that reality, but they are, rightfully, protective. Not everyone makes the cut.

Julia Cameron refers to the people who mess with our reality as "crazymakers," and you can find crazymakers anywhere, including in your band, under your roof—or inside your own head. They're people who always seem to interrupt you when they see you're working, people who want to party on the night your ensemble rehearses, people with a "catastrophe" and a two-hour phone call every night. Intentionally or not, they pull us off course and away from our missions, goals, and dreams.

When we cut crazymakers out, space is created, and better choices fill that space. We find people who know that time is short and that there's so much to do. They don't have to be in music at all—they just have to be true Top Right Quadrant people (*I trust you/you are trustworthy*).

Two tips:

1. When you find the good ones, *do not let them get away.*
2. The best way to find the good ones is to *be* one of the good ones.

As for the crazymakers, you know who they are. Get your journal and write their names down. Crazymakers have themselves to deal with. *Let them.*

We've got work to do.

Fifteen

TROUBLESHOOTING

In the back of appliance manuals, there's usually a "Troubleshooting" section. I love when my problem is listed; it feels so fixable. I feel less alone.

Trouble: Toastmaster™ does not make toast.

Troubleshoot:
1. Check that Toastmaster™ is plugged into a working outlet.
2. After inserting bread, check that you have depressed SIDE LEVER until it clicks.
3. If untoasted bread does not descend into Toastmaster™, check for blockage. WARNING: DO NOT STICK METAL OBJECTS OF ANY KIND INTO TOASTMASTER™.

That's what this section is. After listening to thousands of songs in progress, I've noticed common spots where things get wonky, and I've offered ideas on how to approach a revision. Hopefully, your problem is here and toast is on the way.

Preparation for Troubleshooting

Here are some suggestions on how to prepare drafts—and yourself— for the critical task of troubleshooting.

1. **Make every viable version.** They are your prototypes that will be beta tested by your troubleshooting process. Don't despair: A lot of prototypes don't work. But they could lead to one that does.

2. *Finish* **all the versions in a way that expresses the intent and flow of a fully realized version**—from a *songwriting* point of view, not a production point of view. That is, don't sweat the EQ on the snare just yet. You can even just record into your phone. We're looking for the big picture.

3. **Get as much time between you and your drafts as you can.** Hopefully, after a while, you'll forget where the stitches are and you can approach the draft with fresh ears, as a first-timer might.

4. **When you've gotten as much distance as you can stand, play your versions in a row, either in recorded form or live, and let them duke it out.** More often than not, the field will self-select, and the most compelling combination(s) of your ideas will push forward.

5. **Yes, I said "combination(s)," with the "s" in parentheses, because you may well resolve that there are different shades to a vision that a single approach can't encapsulate.** Is one "best"? Or are they all explorations of something more mysterious? Are your different versions just you turning a strange artifact around in your hands? (And isn't that *exactly* what you'd do if you came across a strange artifact?) Must you arrive at a definitive version of something you yourself might not even fully understand?

   The more I listen, the more I think the entire concept of the "definitive version" is just capitalism—the need for a label to own the "master" recording—getting in our heads. We are allowed to give more than one opinion, and perhaps even conflicting opinions, on what we've found.

We already do this, of course, and technology has helped facilitate it. We call these other "opinions" the remix. Or the alternate take. Or the radio edit. Or the club version. Or the chill study mix. Any one of these could be The One. Just talk to a true fan: Their favorite version could be the one from a ski lodge when "there were like five people in the place, *and I was one of them.*" Or "the live set from the Village Vanguard, 1964, man." Or "the Tiny Desk version on NPR." Ask a Grateful Dead fan about their favorite take of "St. Stephen" and settle back, because that's like asking for a half-hour history lesson on the '72 tour.

We might not even be the one to capture the definitive version *of our own work.* My favorite version of Leonard Cohen's "Hallelujah" is k.d. lang's, sung at the 2010 Winter Olympics in Vancouver. Lana Del Rey has injected songs from Gershwin's "Summertime" to Sublime's "Doin' Time" with her own dreamlike sensibility. The central mystery inside a great song can even be shared: A standard like "My Way," to me, contains both Frank Sinatra and Sid Vicious. I can hear Sid's snarl in Frank's version and Frank's egoism in Sid's. And I can hear our collective human fatalism in both; a song is larger than any artist who performs it.

Does this make troubleshooting harder or easier? Both! So, sure, search for a "definitive take," but maybe accept how limited that is—even if you wrote it.

On to Troubleshooting

Here are some problem areas that we discuss a lot in class:

Trouble: The Intro Is Not Sure What It's Introducing Yet

The intro is an opportunity—meaning it's not a prerequisite. Sometimes, writers will give a simple two-bar cycle that sets the verse up, and that works fine, but I've noticed that a lot of intros are arrived at by default, and they can feel that way. The writer needed some kind of first-draft launchpad, but as we know from space travel, a successful rocket doesn't take the launchpad with it.

Troubleshoot:

1. **Don't touch it. It's perfect.** Your first idea was your best idea. You simply wanted to establish the tempo and the arrangement. It's genius. You're a genius.

2. **Cut it. Entirely.** *If it's not improving on silence, then don't say it.* Start at the verse, or the chorus, or whatever is exciting. The song literally needs no introduction, and the result is a sense of immediacy—the listener is thrown right into the pool, clothes, cocktail, and all.

3. **Open with an instrumental taste of the chorus but save the chorus lyric for later.** See Nirvana's "Smells Like Teen Spirit," but, better, see old-timey Broadway shows that begin with an overture that stacks the melodic high points of *the entire two-and-a-half-hour show* into one pummeling combination of haymakers. Every chorus excerpt is a delicious taste of what's coming, and a compelling reason to stay. Broadway grew out of vaudeville, and it is not shy about doing whatever it takes to keep asses in chairs.

4. **Maybe your intro is genius, but the genius needs a haircut.** Is the eight-bar intro really four? Is the four really two? Is the two really a half-bar drum fill? Is the half-bar drum fill really just a single chord (see the Beatles' "A Hard Day's Night")? Is

the single chord necessary, or can we just get straight to it (see 2, above)? True to my biases, I usually suggest the smallest launchpad *that will also ensure a successful launch*. To twist an old phrase: Don't bore us, get to the song.

5. **Poke around the song draft for something representative, or worthy of repetition, or just cool.** You might not have had these options earlier, but you do now. Maybe your ideas have spun out into an interesting bridge. Take a piece of it—just a hint, don't give us the farm—and start there. If you do, your first verse will arrive fresh because it will be the first time we've heard it, and your bridge will arrive as *repeated information* because it will be the second time we've heard it. (Opening with the chorus does this, too. And it's more chorus, faster.)

6. **What is the coolest *single element* in your song/band/ arrangement?** Is it the bass line? The post-chorus? A drum pattern? A sample? Do you have a hype man? (Not kidding.) Do you like beach sounds or ASMR sound effects? Whatever you've got, clear everything else out of the way and lead with it. Give it a "solo," in other words, and surprise us into listening to the rest. Classic rock example: Led Zeppelin's guitarist/ producer Jimmy Page gave drummer John Bonham the opening bars of "When the Levee Breaks" and turned a seven-minute Brit-blues jam into a high point of the band's catalog. Bonham was superhuman, and Page was smart to spotlight him. Is there someone/something like that in your orbit?

Conclusion: Don't start us off with a preset. Don't sleepwalk us into your song. Forty-eight-bar overture? Fine. Voice memo of an ex screaming at you? Good luck in court, but okay, at least the listener won't be bored. Make it worth it. Whatever it is.

Trouble: The First Line Doesn't Know How Important It Is

A good first line is an invitation addressed to our curiosity. It's the tip of an iceberg of indeterminate size: Where are we in time? Place? Who's the "you"? What's the problem? *Is* there a problem? Are there stakes? What's the relationship of the listener to the story (if there is one)? What's the relationship of the listener to the *vocalist*? Every cultural cue we get from conversation, we get in this opening line. We get accents, language, *relationship* to language, geography, vocal technique, point of view, mood—and all these questions are raised while gesturing toward the entryway doors.

Check that playlist you made earlier in the book. Take a look at the first lines of the songs you chose. Do they pull you in? Do they give a beautiful image, or an imperative verb, or an idea that is loaded with possible interpretation? I'm going to guess yes. Writing by implication is exciting and efficient. We don't get many words in a song, so if just a few can imply many more, we're ahead of the game.

It's understandable, as the writer, if you feel a special attachment to a first line in a song draft—it may have been the launchpad for the whole idea, but you might have outgrown it. And you may need to let it go. Revision is not for the sentimental. It's "troubleshooting:" the "shooting" of "trouble." There will be blood. Like, a *lot of blood*.

Troubleshoot:

1. **As you're writing forward, you may trip over a great metaphor, an evocative image, or an establishing point of view. Pop it into that first line.** So often, my students and I will recognize the better first line, or the better title, hiding elsewhere in the song. Identifying it and then spotlighting it somewhere—moving it to the first line or repeating it in the chorus—sharpens the song's focus and energizes its meaning.

2. **How about opening with the chorus, this time *with* lyric?** This way, the culminating high point of your song is also the first thing the listener hears. So. Try that?

3. **Write a line that implies that something big is on the way, *if* you stick around.** A dubious example is a clickbait headline that lures us with chum like, "Ten Things You're Doing Wrong in the Kitchen. *Number Five Shocked Me.*" "I Never Thought My Dating App Could Do . . . *This.*" We hate clickbait because the resulting article doesn't pay off. The good news is that we don't have to lie like that, but we do have to get a listener to stick around. A beautiful bridge is of no help if no one makes it that far. Many professional pop songwriters don't even bother writing a bridge until they know the rest of the song is strong enough to ensure the listener will get there. A loaded first line will help.

Trouble: The Key Isn't Doing the Song Justice

The intent of the song can change dramatically, depending on the balance of the key it's in and the way the singer inhabits that key. What I mean is: If the singer is stretching for notes, we stretch along with her, and the intent of the lyric fills with that kind of out-of-the-comfort-zone energy. That can be great—if that's what you're looking for. Being in a comfortable key is not always where the intent of the song is best served. This can be hard if *you're* the singer who'll be doing the stretching. What can I say? Maybe it's time to stretch.

Troubleshoot:

1. **Demo the song in different keys.** Listen to it. Live with it for a while. This is really a trial-and-error kind of thing. If you're writing to pitch to other singers, they may have to go through the same process.

2. **The key can also shift, of course.** You may like the energy of one section when it's in one key and the way a different section sits in a different key. Your job, then, may be to work out the connective tissue between two or more keys. Don't be daunted by the idea. See it as a challenge. Many of your favorite songs do this. Some songs like to make a big deal out of it, while others slide in and out unnoticed.

If you listen intently to your revision(s), you may trip over a moment when the song will take over and complete itself, and you'll find yourself changing keys and doing things you never set out to do. Those are exciting moments, like collaborating with ghosts.

Trouble: The Tempo Is Nudging the Song in a Less Compelling Direction

The same song at a different tempo is a completely different song. (See Marilyn Monroe's slowed-down "Happy Birthday" as an extreme example.) A few beats per minute one way or another, and we sensitive little humans color in emotional shades like sarcasm, denial, or eroticism. The time line will expand or contract, causing the words to stack together or spread apart over greater distances. Silence is added or subtracted. Urgency, or lack of it, is implied. In a way, you can mess with a listener's anxiety levels by doling out musical information at different speeds.

Troubleshoot:
1. **Challenge the tempo at which the song first came to you.** Play it fast, play it slow, notice what happens in each scenario. You can find a whole new interpretation of a song by doing this.
2. **Allow the tempo to drift naturally, without a "click track" or metronome.** Digital workstations are set up on a "grid" that

institutes a rigid tempo for a project, and the intent of the song may fight against that. This wasn't always the way. Before the days of the click track, songs would breathe along with the musicians and the energy of sections. Some still do, but most have surrendered the concept of time to our computer over-lords. Depending on what kind of music you make, you might want to work "off the grid." That phrase makes it sound kind of survivalist, and I don't know, maybe it is? What survives is the human interpretation of time.

3. **If that's too much, you might try programming a drift in tempo into those computers.** A song that you start at 120 beats per minute might end at 122, causing a subconscious acceleration of energy that reads as "excitement." Or the cho-ruses might slow a little and sit in a pocket that the verse sec-tions don't benefit from.

Nothing is cheating. If a parameter can be tweaked, everyone's tweaking it. All the time. In a thousand ways.

Trouble: The Writer Is Using a Less Interesting Point of View

Example:

> *You* feel so alone
> *You've* got no one to talk to
> *You* just can't believe that no one sees the good in *you*
> And *you* don't think *you* can make it through

A potentially heart-wrenching verse is set in second person. This disembodies both the subject of the song ("you," meaning "one") and the narrator, who has a God's-eye view of "your" feelings. Suspicious!

> I feel so alone
> I've got no one to talk to
> I just can't believe that no one sees the good in me
> And I don't think I can make it through

Which one is more vulnerable? Which is more compelling? Which one do I need to cry-sing along with when I'm alone on my ratty plaid couch in my underwear clutching an open tequila bottle, desperate that time is passing with nothing to show for it? I think you know.

Sometimes the distance is necessary, and sometimes you really did want the God's-eye view, but I rarely see a song get worse when it gets more intimate.

Troubleshoot:

1. **Give yourself a talking to.** When you wrote, "He-e-e . . . will always love . . . the-e-em," did you really mean, "*I-I-I* will always love *you-u-u*"? Probably, yes. So be brave and say it.

2. **Point of view is a parameter, so try a few out.** In third person, it's going to be a story song with characters working through whatever landscape you choose for them. In first person, it becomes confessional. In the imperative, you might have a Mission Song on your hands ("Keep the Faith," "Fight the Power," and so on).

3. **Time is another parameter to check in with.** In present tense, the narrator is in the midst of the issue. The past, future, or conditional tenses are all going to shade the song differently. Try them. Demo them, then put them next to each other and let them fight it out. More often than not, when you hit the right combination of point of view and time, you'll know. And the more you do this kind of exercise, the sharper your instincts

will get. There is no substitute for experience, which makes finishing songs as important an exercise as starting them.

Trouble: The Idea of the Song Shows Up Late

Verse one, turns out, was a lovely setup, but the song has outgrown it. You're not to blame because you were writing into an idea not knowing what was coming next. You are, however, to blame for leaving it there.

Troubleshoot:

1. **Pop verse two up to verse one.** This might mean discarding verse one and writing a new verse two that expands on the knowledge you gained in (your new) verse one. There's a second opportunity here, which is to do what Shane McAnally suggested and take verse two somewhere completely new and different.

2. **Try simply flipping the verses.** In this revision, the (new) verse one drops us into the heart of the story, while the (new) verse two gives setting and background that we can now contextualize because, thanks to (new) verse one, we know where the song is going. When this works, it can change the time line of events and deepen the intent of the song. This is a common technique in journalism: At the very top of an article, the reader is thrown into heavy gunfire, and at around paragraph three, she finds out who the hell's doing the shooting. John McPhee discusses this in his book *Draft No. 4*—linear chronology is only one of many methods of storytelling. So, if you're singing about a murder, you might want to start at the funeral, then cycle back to the crime.

Trouble: The Writer Runs Out of Gas on the Back Half of the Chorus or Song

I hate golf as much as the next sane person, but one thing I've noticed is that "golf people" talk a lot about follow-through. I'll give them this: Follow-through is key.

Sometimes, a kick-ass opening to a chorus draft will be followed either by a mad sprint to *get the hell out of the chorus* or by the more compliant *the first part was great, so just repeat it until it feels chorus-length.* In a way, this type of chorus is almost a metaphor for the writing process itself: Inspiration might get you only part of the way there, even if you just want to go eight bars.

Here's a dumb-as-rocks litmus test for whether you have a gassed-out chorus: *Are you bored?* If you're bored, we're probably bored. *Don't bore us.* Get to the back half of the chorus.

Troubleshoot:

1. **Leave it alone.** You minimalist genius, you. You might even double its length in subsequent choruses, but that's it. If you have only one thing to say, it helps to make that the *only* thing you say.

2. **Follow through on the back half with complementary ideas, contrasting melodies, or a twist on the arrangement.** I'm being vague because your options are limitless. Again: Consult the playlist you made in the early chapters and check out the choruses. I bet they "pay off" in a satisfying way.

3. **Chart out the shape of a chorus you love.** A tidy pop chorus might be constructed like a miniature song in itself, with a statement, a move away from it, and a satisfying return to it. The focus of this particular revision is to write that compelling move away from the initial idea . . . *so that you can return to it,* fresh, shining, and edified. Triumphant! In short: We have to

go away in order to return, and your chorus may want to set up the satisfaction of that return to the familiar centering image. Sometimes knowing exactly what we want to say isn't enough, in this context. We have to say it, then *take it away*, then say it again so the listener will really appreciate it. Has this scenario happened to you in other, non-songwriting parts of your life? Oh, I'm sure it has. And I hope you've journaled about it.

Note: The same thoughts apply to the back half of the song. You've set up your brain puzzle in the first half; in the back half, subvert the rules you've set up. Vary the themes. Bridges do this well. Solos or arranger's moments do, too. Try a breakdown chorus or jerk the wheel and take the song into an entirely different tempo and feel. (See: Billie Eilish, "Bad Guy.") Or again: Add by subtraction and cut, cut, cut.

Trouble: The Song Is Trying to Tell Two Stories at Once

When you tell two at once, you tell neither well. Symptoms include an inconsistent point of view, or a shift in tense, or, in dire cases, a post-song disclaimer/explainer, which is when the songwriter goes on for five minutes after the song is over to explain that another narrator showed up and took over, but the listener didn't *know* that because it happened behind the scenes, in between the post-chorus and verse two . . . it can get complicated.

The problem with the post-song disclaimer/explainer is that you won't be around to deliver it every time the song plays. So, if everyone in the room is confused, there's probably work to be done.

Troubleshoot:

1. **Leave it.** Your whole point was to be elliptical, enigmatic, eclectic, other things that start with "e," and you've hit the mark. Songs *shouldn't* make sense, and you're not obligated

to mean *anything*. In *How to Be an Artist*, Jerry Saltz writes, "The faster your work makes sense, the faster people will lose interest," and many agree, including you. Besides, we never hear the same song twice, anyway: Its meaning changes as we change, and as the world changes around us. *We have no control of meaning.* End of revision.

2. **Split the draft into separate, clearer drafts.** This advice bums people out because it turns one "finished" song into two unfinished fragments. But: Two more shots at a great song! Maybe even two great songs! Can you imagine if we were built like those underwater creatures that can duplicate themselves when their body parts get lopped off? King Solomon could have advised, "You know? Just cut the kid in half. And look: two kids!" Am I calling myself King Solomon right now? *Yes. Yes I am. Cut the child in half. And look: two beautiful children. You're welcome.*

3. **Find the one, bigger story that connects the two orphaned stories.** What you find could end up being a new chorus that unifies the two stories you've been telling. In the way that any note can work in any key, any story can coexist—sometimes, the further apart the stories appear, the more satisfying the union will wind up being. The work here is in finding that through-line and spotlighting it.

Trouble: The Writer Is Bending Syllables to Fit the Melody

Example: There's a peanut butter named Smooth Operator, manufactured by Peanut Butter & Co., and I am fanatically loyal. It's not the easiest peanut butter to find, but I know the stores that sell it, and that's where I go.

The *only* problem with Smooth Operator is that I can't pronounce the name correctly because pop singer Sade stressed the third syllable of "operator" on her 1984 hit of the same name. Now, when I pull a jar from the shelf at Key Food, I sing the title setting just like she did: *Op-er-AAA-torrr*. It's become my first full-on, self-penned Dad Joke, and I've grown addicted to my family's disgust. And yes, I sing directly to the jar, but I do *not* make believe the jar is a microphone. That's stupid.

Calling out syllables that are sung differently than they're spoken isn't about traditionalism. It's about focusing your audience's attention. Anything that plays with a natural flow should be worth the attention it gets. *Can* an interruption be worth it? Absolutely. Mis-stressed syllables can be a great sound effect. And Sade certainly didn't seem to suffer for it. But I think it's worth putting a move like that to a stringent test just to make sure it doesn't come off as lazy or simply an ineffective use of the spotlight.

Am I overreaching? Probably. Like bent rhymes, bent syllables can actually work out to be a hook simply *because* they stick out a little—*op-er-AAA-torrr*—so maybe that's a win? If Sade had pronounced the word "correctly," would I have forgotten the song completely? Would I be buying a different peanut butter? Perhaps we'll never know.

Troubleshoot:

1. **Don't touch it.** You love what it says and how it says it. Never trust a man who'd go on for two paragraphs about his peanut butter.

2. **Prioritize the melody, subjugate the lyric.** Play the song again but sing "la" in place of the lyric you have. When you have a solid melody, get the words to sing the way they're spoken, without changing the meaning of the section or the intent of the song. Prioritizing the melody requires extra facility with lyric writing. I have found that writing melody is a more instinctive and organic process. It comes from a wordless

place. When the lyric serves the melody, the song can feel connected to its primary source.

Trouble: The Song Is Too Long

Feedback like, "Your song's so short!" can actually be seen as a compliment. The listener wanted more. That's good! On the other hand, hearing, "Your song is so long!" is *never* a good thing. Why? Because they wanted less. At some point, the song did not improve on silence.

In class, unless a song is clearly unfinished, I rarely suggest adding sections, and more often recommend getting out the scissors to do some (more) cutting.

Troubleshoot:

1. **Shorter = better.** How much shorter? Until you stop improving on silence. Caveat: An EDM writer played me a song, and I suggested cutting an eight-bar section in half. He said he couldn't because that would yield a four-bar phrase that would screw up other DJs who might incorporate the song into their sets. In this case, cutting the section down, while possibly good for the song, would be bad for the song's utility in that specific genre. Is that a cynical choice? I don't judge. Technology and art are constantly in conversation. And it goes both ways: Compact discs were supposedly made to hold seventy four minutes of music so they could fit all of Beethoven's Ninth Symphony. So, score one for art.

2. **Farm your long song, harvest many songs.** You're bristling with ideas, can't help yourself, verse five is where the subplot really takes off, you took two guitar solos because you had two totally indispensable guitaristic opinions, and the background

singer really went off in one part, so that had to stay, and . . . and . . . and . . .

And editing is hard. But you can console yourself by giving each jewel of an idea its own tiara, where it can shine.

Trouble: The Writer Hasn't Separated What Actually Happened from What a Song Can Convey Best

I'll suggest lyrical changes for students and hear, "Yeah, but that's not what really happened." This may sound harsh, but *no one cares* what really happened. We're not in court, and your song is not admissible. Your song sits in the fiction section of whatever library you envision. "Fiction" doesn't mean it isn't true, by the way. It might be even truer.

Troubleshoot:

1. **Serve the song, not the facts.** If her car has to be red instead of yellow because you need a one-vowel color to make a line work, paint the dang car red. Switch "he" and "she" and take the better arrangement of fictional cast members in your song. *You* know what really happened. The *listener* wants the best song regardless what really happened.

2. **Serve the facts and teach them.** Sometimes saying what actually happened is the most empowering—and universal— choice you can make. Example: In response to the 2020 killing of George Floyd by a Minneapolis police officer, artists wrote protest songs that called on listeners to "say his name" in order to keep it—and the outrage—alive.

   By inserting the facts into a rallying cry, the songwriter *teaches* them to the listener using all the tools songwriting brings to bear: repetition, rhyme, melody, rhythm, community, and so on.

Trouble: The Song Is Using an Ill-Fitting Form

Two sections of equivalent "weight" are connected by something that sounds like a pre-chorus and tries to rise but has nowhere to rise to because the song lands at a place of equivalent weight again. Writers who watch the charts often try to force ideas into the verse-chorus form, but that just doesn't always pan out. Better: Write your best song in the form that suits it.

Troubleshoot:

1. **Leave it.** You're just that original, and history will eventually catch up to you.
2. **Try the song in another form.** Which one? Well, how many good sections do you have? Try using only them. That will limit your options considerably.

   By this I mean: Does the song you're writing have a central thought, or mission, or image that seems to tie everything together? If so, that might be what you need to set within a complementary form.

   - If it's one white-hot thought, you may have the engine of a chorus.
   - If there are two thoughts engaged in conversation ("Yesterday" and "Somewhere Over the Rainbow" come to mind), you may have an AABA, or two-section, form.
   - An overarching line that summarizes several ideas and acts almost like a mantra? Could be a refrain for an AAA.

3. **Trial and error.** Trial and f*&%ing error.

Trouble: The Song Has a Rickety Bridge

This is the bridge that's just the last line of the chorus sung a few different ways as a refrain. Sometimes on lyric sheets it'll look like this:

Oooh (8×)

Pro songwriters don't always write bridges because (1) it's not a chorus; (2) if you didn't like the chorus, why bother, no one will ever hear it; and (3) if they can get a recording artist to record the song, the artist can write the bridge and justify taking a preposterous cut of the publishing in exchange for the star power they bring to the table.

Troubleshoot:
1. **Leave it. It's wonderful.** You're wonderful. It's a moment to feel, to dwell within the arrangement, so just let that happen.
2. **Write a bridge that gives another perspective on the story you're telling.** It can be a clarification, a counterargument, a cameo from a completely different artist. Bridges can include lyrics but obviously don't *have* to. Instrumental arranger's bridges can imply layers of a song that language can't reach. Or they can just let us live in the abstract emotional space of the song for a while. They can be mini-vacations that are matched only by, well, by silence.
3. **If it's not improving on silence, cut it.**

Trouble: The Outro Goes AWOL

Outros can be clearinghouses for all the ideas that didn't make it into the song form: wanky solos, drum fills, vocal histrionics, endless space jams that linger like guests who aren't getting the hint that the party's over.

Troubleshoot:
1. **Keep it.** Whatever your music is getting people to do is something they want to keep doing. Dancing, running, chilling, sexing—you know. Don't kill the vibe. *Be* the vibe. *Extend* the vibe. (But do a radio edit, too.)

2. **Cut it.** Huge pop songs over the past decade end at the very last note of the final chorus. Which approach best serves your context? These are questions that instinct and practice will answer. Hopefully, the deciding vote will come from the song and not you and *definitely* not from the horn player who's lobbying to extend the song because he played some cool stuff toward the end.

3. **Fade it.** Just hear me out: At the moment of this writing, fades are so out of fashion that when a student uses one, they get applause from the classroom for the audacity.

   I love what a fade-out implies—that whatever is happening in the song continues on without you, as if it were a carnival leaving town. You can only watch and wave as it ambles down the highway. I use the verb "watch" deliberately because there's a very visual quality to the fade, as if the slow deprivation of hearing urges the brain to engage our other senses. The term itself—"fade"—is borrowed from film, which originated around the same time as recorded music.

   Fades can imply continuity—the song goes on forever—as easily as loss—the song goes on forever *without you*. They do this by reintroducing us to the universal language of silence, which becomes part of the meaning of the song. Fades remind us that silence always gets the last word.

Pro/Con of Fades:
- **Pro:** Shortens the song; you don't have to write an ending; alludes to human impermanence (in the good way?).
- **Con:** Possibly gimmicky; doesn't assert the end of a song; too psychedelic; doesn't answer the question of an ending when played live. (If you perform, you're going to have to write an ending anyway, so you might as well do it now.)

How It Ends

They say, "You never get a second chance to make a first impression," but you don't get a second chance to make a last impression, either. Consider a cowboy sauntering through a saloon's double doors, and three minutes later getting tossed out the window in a shower of bullets and broken glass. Now picture that same cowboy sauntering back out in a top hat, carrying a bride over the saloon's threshold in a shower of confetti and fireworks. One event informs the other, and both are opportunities to frame what happened in the interim.

With that in mind, I decided to speak with Jim Anderson, producer and sound engineer; former president of the Audio Engineering Society; multi-Grammy Award–winner; and professor at New York University's Clive Davis Institute. His office features several Grammy statues and an espresso machine. We talked fades.

What causes someone to decide on a fade?

I think sometimes the song kind of tells you what it wants to do at the end. Sometimes you really don't have an ending, or you just want to vamp and let it go. Years ago, I observed [bassist] Jaco Pastorius recording the *Word of Mouth* album at [New York City recording studio] Power Station. It was Jack DeJohnette [drums], Herbie Hancock [keys], Toots Thielemans [harmonica], and a room full of brass players and all that kind of thing. And I heard Jaco say to the engineer, "What we're going to do is, when we get to the end of the chart, they're going to vamp and I'm going to leave the room. And one of two things is going to happen: We're going to run out of tape; or the whole thing will just fall apart, and that'll be my fade." It's another bow in the quiver—another artistic choice people can make.

To what degree did fades come from the limitations of the studio—the wax rolls, tape reels, and such?

Well, popular music was always being dictated by the medium or by the technology. So, if you had a cylinder or a 78, you were always limited to two and a half, three minutes. If the song went on beyond that, you *had* to fade. Then they developed the slightly ultrafine groove—Edison came up with this—so you could get about four minutes on a cylinder. But when the 45 came out, you were still kind of locked into something in the neighborhood of two and a half to three minutes. And so on.

Are there fades that predate technology?

The first one that I'm aware of, and it's fairly famous, is the Haydn Symphony No. 45 ["Farewell," 1772]. Basically the story was that Haydn and his musicians were held longer than anticipated [at patron Prince Nikolaus Esterházy's Hungarian summer palace], and they wanted to go home and be with their families. So, Haydn wrote an extra movement after the piece: Every musician played their part, and when they were done, they'd blow out the candle on their music stand and leave the stage. Eventually, all that was left were two violinists sitting there, and [Esterházy] got the hint.

Kind of the opposite of how a bar will turn the house lights on at the end of the night.

Yeah, you know—lights on, and out come the vacuum cleaners, and it's time to go.

Parting Shot

These troubleshooting issues are just some of what I've witnessed in my classes and my time teaching. These are the golf swings I try to correct most often. If I taught at other schools, I might have a completely different list for you. My guess is that a different list would amount to dozens of different ways to say, "Pack more better ideas into a smaller package."

Happy 'shooting.

Sixteen

WRITER'S BLOCK

Here's the thing about writer's block: *There's no such thing.* It doesn't exist. It's the Bigfoot of artistic maladies. Like Bigfoot, it's got a great name—it just *sounds* real, the way scarlet fever sounds plush and velvety instead of being the lousy rash it is.

The word "block" implies there's a big chunk of *something* separating you from your songwriting . . . *but there isn't.* Sure, physical blocks are possible. If, say, you were walking by a building and an air conditioner slipped out of an eighth-floor window and landed on you: legitimate block. If you had one of those aphasias you read about in Oliver Sacks's books where patients are totally normal except they have no recognition of vowels anymore: legit. If you're wearing mittens and can't play chords: fine.

But that's it. We are not "blocked" from writing. *We invented an affliction.*

Well, *we* didn't. "Writer's block" is a term that was coined in the 1940s by Dr. Edmund Bergler, an Austrian Freudian psychiatrist who lived exactly where you'd expect to find an Austrian Freudian psychiatrist: New York City.

Bergler blamed writer's block on some seriously Freudian suspects: "milk-denying mothers" mostly, but also mental states that include the words "anal," "phallic," "oral," "abortive"—you get it. In a savage review of his book *The Writer and Psychoanalysis*, *Time* magazine asked, "What compulsion makes a man set out to explain most of the world's literature as just an infant's whimper for a bountiful teat[?]" But criticism waned, and the concept, like Bigfoot, survived.

I would pick through more of Bergler's findings (funny how everything sounds Freudian now), but I'm just going to cut to the spoiler: *There is a cure for the invented affliction known as writer's block*. After thousands of pages written on this topic, the lab-coated studies, the academic papers, the peer-reviewed research, the post-graduate dissertations, the cure is, are you *ready*:

Write through it.

That's it. I'm sorry it wasn't something more exotic, but ironically, the cure for the disease is to ignore the disease and do what you'd be doing if you didn't have it. You read that right: *The treatment is the same, whether you have it or not.* And this same conclusion is reached from a thousand different directions:

> Here's Scott Barry Kaufman, scientific director of the University of Pennsylvania's Imagination Institute: "It's good to just keep putting things down on paper—ideas, knowledge, etc."
> Here's Jhumpa Lahiri: "If one sticks to a schedule and tries to write on a regular basis, something will eventually come."
> Here's Maya Angelou: "What I try to do is write."
> Here's what's on the last page of *The War of Art* by Steven Press-field: "Do it or don't do it."
> Here's Yoda, in the Dagobah swamp: "Do or do not. There is no try."

If you're not going to listen to Yoda, you're not going to listen to me. But we're saying the same thing. So take it from him. Whatever.

Write through it.

So, If It's Not Writer's Block, What Is It?

It's fear. And, unlike "writer's block," fear is definitely legitimate.

Poet Mary Ruefle refers to fear as the "ghost of our experiences," which I think includes the ghost of evolution, meaning, yes, we're haunted by things that happened to us, but we're also haunted by millions of years' worth of things that *didn't* happen to us. We carry around the burden of instincts that we wield like phantom limbs we're still trying to use.

Fear has been very helpful—we've gotten this far, after all—but we can afford to practice some of it out of us. It can be done. Example: If I'm on a park bench with a muffin and a cup of coffee, pigeons and squirrels will come right up to me and play the odds that I'm not suddenly going to drop my muffin and skewer one of them. They're always right, and their lack of fear is reinforced every time they live through a visit with me. I can even share that park bench with humans who are covered head to toe in pigeons and will gladly pose for pictures. There's a total breakdown of fear between species, and we're amazed by it—hence the pictures. Call it "domestication" or "symbiosis"—pigeon gets food crumbs, person gets fame crumbs—but either way, it's a reminder that animals can alter their biological responses. So can we.

What Are We Afraid Of?

So much. *So, so much.* I've met students who are afraid of failure *and* success simultaneously. There's a fear of being seen and a fear of being ignored, fear of being too different and of being a living cliché. One student told me that, at age nineteen, it was too late for him to learn how to arrange horns. Another told me that she couldn't write a Mission Song because she was from New Jersey, and who'd be interested in *that*? (She knew Bruce Springsteen, after I reminded her, but then feared that Jersey was "over" because someone had already done it.)

Fear seems like it helps us identify danger, but in assigning danger to anything we don't understand, fear's evolutionary default is *hide*. In this moment, fear freezes us until we can figure out what's next; often, what's next is, "Keep hiding (preferably in a pack)." Fighting this instinct to hide is a distinctly anti-pack move, and as we said earlier, we owe our hierarchy on the food chain to working in packs.

The problem for us as songwriters is that "fear" is in our job description. That's what we're asking ourselves to do—to be afraid and then to walk with and *work with* that fear. Or, to turn it around: our job is to be brave.

Can You Write *Without* Fear?

Sure—birthday cards, TV theme songs, Post-it note reminders to floss—I've done all of those, and they can be appreciated, remunerative, and hygienic. Pop music can be all about fun. Here's a prompt: Write fun songs and work out your fears somewhere else. Go to therapy, or swallow swords, or something.

What About Droughts?

Droughts, slumps, ruts—whatever you want to call them—are a whole different ballgame. They aren't writer's block, because you *are* writing, and they aren't fear, because you're not afraid—they're you, being you, and not liking you. It's a crappy feeling, and it happens, but—hear me out—droughts can be good news, too.

Here are a few typical droughts my students have contended with, and how to flip them in your favor.

"I Have Nothing to Say"

First of all: Nah. I don't believe it. Even a dog tied up outside the grocery store has something to say. A *lot*, actually. You may be tired, drained, or prioritizing elsewhere.

Question: What do you do when the gas tank is empty? You roll to a stop and die wherever you land, right? Wrong. You fill the tank. As a writer, you just may need to fill the tank by taking some inspiration in. Any kind of art is gas in the tank. Exercise, vacuuming out the car, or just meditating to clear your mind are also good ideas. Here's another: Consider service to others. Not for selfish reasons but because everything is connected to who you are, not just as a writer but as a person and a citizen. The irony is that when you work selflessly, so much more comes back to you. Teaching and mentoring has done this for me, and it's not because it helps me write; it helps me live, and the writing is part of that living.

This is all very different than having nothing to say.

"What I'm Writing Sucks"

You have no idea if it sucks because, until it's done, you don't even know what it is. The person telling you it sucks is the editor in your head—not the writer. The writer writes; the editor shuts up until the writer is done writing. Once the writer is done, the editor gets to talk.

You might not even *understand* what you're writing yet. If you're anything like me, your subconscious doesn't draw a straight line. An outlier song today could be a signature song tomorrow. Sometimes the subconscious leaps forward first, and the conscious plays catch-up. When writing is a ritual part of your day, you become used to this dynamic. Ritual is a trick, like a trance intended to get you out of your own way. It's yet another benefit of repetition.

"I'm Bored with What I Write"

Maybe, but if you ask me, I'd bet you're *on the threshold of a breakthrough.*

You may have seen this script on home improvement shows on TV: a pasty couple gets bored with their pantry, they whine to a spiky-haired host with a tape measure, and fifteen minutes later, they've got marble countertops, a kitchen island with barstool seating, and a new baby on the way.

What lit the fuse? *Boredom.*

Boredom is the dissatisfied mind reaching outward and not finding anything—*yet.* Boredom, when amplified, becomes frustration; frustration, when amplified, creates change. These are all energized places to be, even though they seem on the surface to be listless and agitated. Boredom is *exciting* because it's a signal that an irreversible chain reaction is imminent and that you're prepared to leap forward into a new style, aesthetic, or mission.

Boredom is a gift! It's an omen from the songwriting gods! So, if you're bored, I say to you, "Congratulations! Something groundbreaking is around the corner."

Fact is, you're *not* bored—you're impatient. You haven't reached the event horizon, yet, but you can already feel the pull of its gravity. It's likely that you'll never be able to return, but it's increasingly obvious that you can't stay, either. All you really know is that boredom has made the present moment uninhabitable by insisting on your answer to the question: *Who will you be, now that you can no longer be you?*

The only way to know is:

Write through it.

"It Shouldn't Be This Hard"

When a product doesn't show its process, we refer to it as "seamless." Great songs are seamless. They're so seamless that we are fooled into believing that's how they showed up. And when that doesn't happen for us, we think it must be because we suck.

Picture your song as a play. Onstage, a brilliant, seamless story is being told; backstage, people are whisper-screaming about torn gowns and lost props. That doesn't mean the process is "hard." That's just what it's like to put on a play.

"I Like the Song, but It Doesn't Fit with My Brand"

This is a twenty-first-century entry into the Pantheon of Drought, accelerated by social media and whatever dividend it implies is forthcoming—influence, ambassadorship, things that sound like money but rarely end up actually being money. My students become paralyzed by the brand image they've worked out on their social media pages and end up throwing out great songs that don't fit, along with all the artistic possibilities they imply. Branding becomes the reason behind not moving forward. Students send themselves to Brand Jail and self-impose a lockdown.

Songwriter Lucy Dacus put it succinctly in an interview in the *Creative Independent*:

> Your brand, or your personality, or whatever you want to call it—it's weird that you would equate the two—it's there already. You have one without trying to have one. So when you're true to that, people respond to it. You don't have to *try* to have a brand. It just exists. . . . If people stopped thinking about what their social media looked like, it would just start to look like them.

To control the brand is to lose control of the personality who thought it up to begin with. It kills me to witness because this idea of "brand" acts like a fixed point, whereas the personality behind it is constantly evolving and shooting out sparks of what it might be next. Brands "pivot"; but people just *move*.

176 Music, Lyrics, and Life

Conclusion

Writer's block doesn't exist. Fear exists but is afraid of its own shadow. Droughts exist but are mislabeled as "bad" when they're really signs we're headed somewhere new. New places trigger our fear responses. And around and around it goes.

If you're a writer, you show up for work, just like everybody else. So, go to work. It's good there. You don't have to love it every day. Find ways to make it fun. Taco Tuesday. Crazy Shirt Thursday. Casual Friday. Mix it up.

But show up, because your boss is looking.

Songwriting Prompt

Several years ago, I enrolled in an "experiential philosophy" program, which I think is a fancy term for "cult." I think it got into a bunch of legal trouble, and some people died during the program. Anyway, it no longer exists, but it was intense, borderline abusive—"tough love" taken to fetish levels.

We were blindfolded a lot and did a good bit of screaming. It wasn't all bad. I hugged strangers, and for a short while, I lost the ability to communicate with language—I decided that words were meaningless, and the "music" of physicality and intent was how we exchanged anything of importance. So I ambled around New York City moaning and scatting at passersby.

My cult had a saying that it put on banners of increasing point size, and every time my blindfold came off, I'd see it in larger and larger lettering: WHAT ARE YOU PRETENDING NOT TO KNOW?

It's kind of accusatory, and weirdly strict, but I guess you expect a little discipline from someone who blindfolds you. I liked that it asked me to face a kind of fear that is self-inflicted. *I'm* pretending not to know. So, *I'm* in control (never mind the blindfold). If I'm the one inflicting the not-knowing, then I'm the one with the power to liberate myself from it.

So: What are *you* pretending not to know?

In other words: What are you afraid of?

What are you afraid of writing about?

What would you admit if you weren't afraid of writing about it?

Each fear that stops you from writing is a writing prompt.

Seventeen

RELATED TIPS FROM UNRELATED FIELDS

Writers who give lists of writing tips are generous—many are teachers—and I'm sure they want to help, but I think they know the futility of step-by-step instructions. So you may see the last tips on those lists advising you to ignore everything you just read. Here are some examples of last tips:

"Break any of these rules sooner than say anything outright barbarous."—George Orwell, "Politics and the English Language"

"Ignore all proffered rules and create your own, suitable for what you want to say."—Michael Moorcock, "Ten Tips for Good Storytelling"

"We're breaking all the rules. Even our own rules. And how do we do that? By leaving plenty of room for 'x' qualities."—Sister Corita Kent/John Cage, "Ten Rules for Students and Teachers"

"Write your story as it needs to be written. . . . I'm not sure that there are any other rules. Not ones that matter."—Neil Gaiman, "Eight Rules of Writing"

"It's all really up to you, but you already knew that and knew everything else you need to know somewhere underneath the noise and the bustle and the anxiety and the outside instructions, including these ones."—Rebecca Solnit, "How to Be a Writer: Ten Tips from Rebecca Solnit"

Some last tips are so self-negating that they're almost empowering (and they're funny):

"Try to leave out the part that readers tend to skip."
—Elmore Leonard, "Ten Rules for Good Writing"

A Theory

Maybe the problem with "lists of writing tips" is that they're too trained on the topic at hand. They're trying to describe the sun by staring straight at it. I think of people like Janna Levin and other cosmologists who never get that kind of satisfaction. They see by implication—not by what something *is* but by how it *acts*.

When *we* see by implication, we get answers that are not "answers" but metaphors that imply a way of thinking. Our question becomes a universal one, and the answer we find reflects us, personally. This sounds particularly useful to a songwriter who's looking to say something universal in a way that hasn't been said before.

So: If we follow anything far enough, it all connects, which means that tips for one thing are really tips for anything. The writers' tips you just read can apply to fixing an appliance, finding your true soul, or crossing the street. Conversely, a list of tips from unrelated fields—particularly the *last tips*—reveal not only what we're doing while writing songs but also what we're doing while living among each other and navigating all of the inexplainableness that surrounds us. Try it:

"The problem will be having enough time to make all the designs that are in your head."—"Ten Things I Wish I Knew About Cookie Decorating" (*The Simple, Sweet Life*)

"Live a healthy life."—"Seven Tips for Getting Pregnant Faster" (*WebMD*)

"Friends can make all the difference: they have warm couches on cold nights, showers, kitchens . . . BUT A CAVEAT! Friends also have their limits." —"Ten Tips for Car Living" (*AnnaOutdoors*)

"K = 2NuP K = u (The Molecular Clock)
You are collecting mutations (data for future anthropologists) right now."—"Five Obscure Formulas that Rule the World" (*Discover*)

"Last but definitely not least: Be nice. You're all on this long flight together so be pleasant to everyone, from the gate agents to your fellow passengers."—"Fifteen Tips for Surviving a Long Flight" (*JohnnyJet*)

George Saunders on Honesty

In general, prose writers are better at "writing about writing" than other artists are, which shouldn't be a shocker: Writing is what writers do.

George Saunders is a prime example. He's a recipient of the MacArthur "genius grant," and his novel *Lincoln in the Bardo* won 2017's Man Booker Prize—and the accolades go on from there. More important (to me, anyway), he also teaches at Syracuse University, and in 2021, he released *A Swim in a Pond in the Rain*, a condensation of his twenty years teaching classic Russian short stories by Chekhov, Gogol, Tolstoy, and Turgenev. Now, when I hear people say things like, "Those who can, do; those who can't, teach," I remember a Saunders-ism: "Unless they can."

You were almost a professional musician . . .

I was kind of a low-level professional musician for a while, and I still play. It was my first artistic love, for sure. But I'm not much of a songwriter, as it turns out, which was a big deal to realize. Whatever distinguishes a good songwriter from a so-so one, I didn't have that. It has something to do with the severity of taste.

What do you look for in a song that you weren't able to provide?

I think it's probably personality. That's actually the big one. In my songs, the first verse is, "I love you so much. You're so beautiful." The second verse is, uh, the same, basically. Or it's the obvious next logical development, and the flavor of response, as I do it, feels reductive. With good songwriters, A and B have such a weird relationship, and that's what makes the brilliance. You are soundly in "A," expecting certain things, and then "B" comes along and is neither too neat nor too out of relation with "A."

It seems odd. I'm just thinking about "story songs," and I feel like you could really nail that.

Here's the thing: I think in all art, the fatal moment is when you're creating something and the reader or listener becomes aware of your agenda. I think the essential thing is honesty—what we might call "compositional honesty." How open are you to changing your plan, in response to what's actually, and maybe inadvertently, happening within the work in progress? If I'm writing a story and I "know" the ending and am holding that ending back to, like, spring it on you, that's dishonest—*I'm prohibiting the story from responding to its own energy.* If the story decides it wants to go somewhere else, I'm not letting it, which leads to little moments of falseness within the narrative. So, for me, the whole thing is picking that apart and saying, "Well, why is it that, when I got to page three, I just checked out?" Or, "Why is it that, on the third repetition of the intro material, I started feeling condescended to just a tiny bit?" It's important for an artist to think about this because the listener can turn off the song. A reader can throw the book across the room.

That may be one of the reasons why songs have gotten shorter: Simply by having gotten to the end, you think it's a better song than it was.

That makes sense. I think a song should go on for only as long as it is truly reacting to itself originally. It should be exactly as long as it needs to be, like what Lincoln said about his legs.

I often quote something you said about the definition of art: "What's important is that something undeniable and nontrivial happens between entry and exit." Can you expand on that?

Early in the process of making a work of art, we tend to have a plan. You're in control of the story, you know where it's going, you know the effect it's going to have, and you proceed. You start applying your taste, line by line. You're cutting or tightening sentences you can't live with. It's almost like if you're driving a car blindfolded but you can feel the wheel will let you turn in one direction and won't let you turn in others. So you just . . . go that way. And then comes a magical moment where you find that you've written (or edited) yourself out beyond that original plan. So you don't know what it is the story is supposed to be doing. And that's a great moment. You just want it to do *something*, and something nontrivial, but you don't have to know exactly what that is.

When I first started writing stories that were good, I noticed that I came out of them going, "What the fuck is that? I don't even know what I just did." Because all I was trying to do is make sure that the energy didn't drop during it. But then the *really* beautiful thing that happened was that those stories meant a lot more than the other ones where I was planning everything.

Mike Tyson once said, "Everybody has a plan until they get punched in the mouth."

That's amazing. A story will definitely punch you in the mouth. The really interesting thing is, can you *truly* not have a plan? I don't think so. But then the process becomes: How do you continually *undercut* the plan? Identify it and then move beyond it? Or, you sense a plan—a shape, a theme, an embedded idea. Do you stand behind that or not? If you don't, you make an adjustment. And, at the end, because you've never been dishonest and you've never let in a banal or needlessly repetitive line and you've never twisted the logic out of its natural shape, your story will spit the reader out on the other end, and she will feel she's been taken on a ride, from where she was before to where she is now. And only then can she kind of go, "What was it that I just went through?"

Excitement is another thing that is so underrated as a state while producing. Now, it's tricky—being excited about what you're writing doesn't guarantee that what you're writing is any good. But I think if you're *not* in that state, it probably presages failure.

You said something about success: "I try not to be full of shit." I thought that was sound advice.

What I mean by that is, there's a sort of systemic falseness in each of us. Revising is having a chance to see evidence of that on the page and then to fix it. So, the place to be not full of shit is while revising.

When I was young and single and we didn't have any kids, I was sort of into the whole idea of having a "persona." I'd just come from Texas to Syracuse, so I had a little bit of an obsession with the West, and Kerouac, and all of that. Given who my heroes were, I kind of thought, "I should probably be a bit of a wild guy." But if you have to *think* that, you're probably not authentically wild. Let's not get confused: I mean, James Joyce was not a pirate. He was James Joyce, and he was James Joyce because he sat at his desk for many, many years.

One of my stated goals was to get the world's attention. And one of the big breakthroughs I had was, I suddenly realized it was okay to freakify your work a little bit in order to get noticed. What I mean by "freakify" is maybe just "urge the story in the direction of originality." So, if you're writing and it sounds a lot like a song by the band you like, that's a problem, maybe. Could you freakify it in some way, to make it not sound like them? Or, ideally, like no one else? Because one, it's going to get you more attention, probably, because it's original, and two, what I found was that the method by which you freakify something is always about you—about your essential artistic urge, your innate taste. Beyoncé's successful because she's really interesting. That's really weird shit that she ends up doing, on *Lemonade*, for example. Everything in it seems to have been radically chosen by her. So . . . if you want to be noticed, try to be noticed. How are you going to be noticed? By being noticeable. Which means: by being more like yourself. And that becomes a technical process—of continually choosing.

You said songwriting was your first artistic love. Knowing that, how did you decide that prose was the better medium for you?

The kind of big principle that I believe in is that, let's say there's twenty things that you do in your life—just general categories of things that you do. We might think we want to be Thing Six. But if we're doing twenty things, and Thing Eighteen is the one that really lights us up, it's a real moment of maturation to say, "My time here is short—what can I do the most beautifully?" I think that's a lesson in prose, but also in life. If you think you're a composer of string quartets, and when you play your string quartets, everybody goes to sleep, and in consolation you pick up your accordion and start playing a polka and everybody dances, well [*laughs*], there you go. There it is.

And to what degree do you think we make that choice?

I think zero.

Zero?

I think.

Agreed.

Eighteen

BEWARE THE IDES OF MYSPACE

By the time this book comes out, whatever I say about technology will be hopelessly out of date. So, let me go the other direction and say:

Do you *know* how many Myspace friends I had?

So many.

They would message me and ask, sometimes angrily, for me to "Top 8" them, which meant adding them to a visible list of my eight besties that Myspace provided on my profile page. Sometimes I would grant their requests—you know, after consideration. I had a music player on my page, and my songs were played a lot. I was living high. Because you know who has followers? *Leaders.*

My point: Do you even know what I'm talking about? How about iLike, MOG, imeem, Makeoutclub, Orkut, Ping, SpiralFrog, Friendster, Shelfari, turntable.fm, Zune, or late epoch organisms like Vine, Google+, StumbleUpon, Klout, Twitter #music, or Yik Yak? These are digital corpses, now splattered like bugs on the windshield of the Wayback Machine.

What happened? The big fish ate the little ones. Myspace ate several. It changed its spelling from MySpace, to Myspace, to myspace, literally shrinking typographically alongside its user base and valuation.

Myspace still makes headlines occasionally: In 2019, it apologized—to whom, I'm not sure—for losing twelve years' worth of music uploads in a "migration error." Charles Darwin would have understood. Hummingbirds, social media platforms—migration is hard. Not everyone survives.

How Does This Relate to Songwriting?

Two ways.

> **Writing:** If you think the above information is archaic, weird, or irrelevant, imagine writing a timeless song and mentioning Blingee'ing your Myspace page. How would the song hold up? Sure, it might work—I love songs about beepers, and T-Birds, and wagon wheels, and steam trains—but tech is a time stamp, and it might keep a universal emotion frozen on a surface level, even if the rest of the song goes deep. If you can, maybe try to avoid writing a heartfelt love song that's in danger of a response like, "Oh, wow, I remember Sony Discmans!"

> **Career:** When we build a fan base on the shifting sands of social media, we become beholden and addicted to that platform. Those platforms have proven, time and again, that (1) they cannot guarantee how long they'll live, and (2) they are not a reliable member of the *team* of your songs. They jiggle their algorithms. They erect tollbooths between our fans and us. They *sell our data*; they bury our gig announcements. Not good!

The best connection we have to our listeners is *whatever the most direct route is.* The fewer middlemen, the better. This is why there's nothing like converting a fan face-to-face at a live show. It's also why platforms offer profile pages and in-app communication *but not email addresses* because that would cut those platforms out of the loop. Marketers know all this, but I'm not talking to marketers. I go to shows all the time. My students call out their Instagram handles— and then it's back to the music.

Get the email addresses or the phone numbers for texting.

Beware the Ides of Myspace.

Songwriting Prompt: What Won't Change?

At re:MARS 2019, Amazon's global artificial intelligence and machine learning event, then-CEO Jeff Bezos was asked what changes he predicted we'd see within the next ten years. He responded, "The bigger question is, 'What's *not* going to change in the next ten years?' Look at what's stable in time and continue to focus there."

Bezos's answer reminded me of a meditation I once learned that asks the practitioner to contemplate God: The definition of God, in this case, is "the part that does not change." Themes of permanence run through the Bible, too. ("For I am the LORD, I change not; therefore ye sons of Jacob are not consumed"—Malachi 3:6.) It's also central to the teachings of Indian guru Paramahansa Yogananda. ("Where motion ceases, God begins.") And Bezos isn't the only Silicon Valley titan who has thought this way: At Apple CEO Steve Jobs's funeral, guests were presented with a brown box containing Yogananda's *Autobiography of a Yogi*. Marc Benioff, CEO of Salesforce and one of Jobs's close friends, said this search for our enduring qualities "was the last thing he wanted us to all think about."

So, let's think about it: What won't change?

Whatever constant is revealed is foundational; it can be built on. Write about *that*.

Nineteen

WALK THE WALK

If left unchecked, songwriting will overtake your life. It will drag you to its lair—the studio, resplendent with toys and couches and delivery menus, devoid of windows or "time," in the conventional sense. It will bend the spine and savage the skin. It will sap the senses and spit out the body. I've seen its victims: sometimes it's hard to discern where "music professional" ends and "comfy chair" begins.

This is not a healthy, or *productive*, consequence of your love of songwriting. Vans and tour buses exacerbate the problem. It's important to remind ourselves to get the hell out of the chair or the passenger seat—and *walk*.

The Pitch

Walking is cheap. It's easy. It doesn't require sweatpants. Or sweat. It's not focused on body-as-brand. It's uninterested in your "best time." It eliminates ambition by erasing not just a finish line but the *relationship* to a "finish line." Walking is about what you saw, not how you looked.

The Privilege

Warning: Anything can meet you on a walk. And by that, I mean each other. Walking is a complex statement—easy as it is to do, you can't do it everywhere, you can't do it whenever you like, and you can't do it with anyone you feel like doing it with. Walking is a method by which we take the temperature of a culture. It's a political act. Racism, sexism, and bias of all kinds are woven into the scenery, like man-made weather patterns. In Garnette Cadogan's essay "Walking While Black," he opens up the "complex and often oppressive negotiation" of walking simply by juxtaposing two quotes and letting them speak:

> "My only sin is my skin. What did I do, to be so black and blue?"
> —Fats Waller, "(What Did I Do to Be So) Black and Blue?"

> "Manhattan's streets I saunter'd, pondering."—Walt Whitman, "Manhattan's Streets I Saunter'd, Pondering"

Here's a song prompt: What would this world look like if anyone could walk anywhere at any time?

The Science

In 2014, Marily Oppezzo and Daniel L. Schwartz of Stanford University decided to figure out if there was a correlation between walking and creativity. The results turned out to be more complex than "Walking = Good." They found that, yes, walking does increase certain types of creative idea generation—a *lot*—but it leaves other important creative mental functions either untouched or even diminished.

Oppezzo and Schwartz concentrated on two types of thinking: "divergent" (the brainstorming, "aha!" moment–making part of the brain) and "convergent" (the reductive ability to interpret and mold the brainstorm once you have one). For us, divergent thinking would be journaling, ideating, crying at the beauty of the sky or the mystery of magnets; convergent is figuring out how to carve a song out of it.

Subjects were tested while seated facing a blank wall, then again on a treadmill set to a comfortable pace, also facing a blank wall. The surprising result was that walking improved the divergent, "aha!" responses but actually *hurt* the ability to think convergently.

In order to understand what was going on, the researchers evaluated the order in which the test was administered. They found that if subjects were tested while seated, then again while walking, creative responses skyrocketed. They *also* found that if subjects were walking first, then seated, they did just as well, indicating that the benefits of walking lingered.

Here's the kicker: If the subjects were seated and stayed seated, *people actually got worse.*

If you're a creative person, it's as if you just heard how to fix the Kentucky Derby.

To find out whether environment played a role in ideation, researchers tried the test outdoors, on a predetermined path. The trend was clearly the same: nature walking and blank-wall walking both gave the divergent benefit. Conclusions: (1) It's the act of walking, not where you walk, that gives the benefit; and (2) Blank walls—not so blank!

Yeah, but Why?

How does someone read into these results? A theory I like is that a divergent mindset might have been important for early hunter-gatherers who walked in search of food. It makes sense that all manner of scheming and strategizing probably happened on those early walking paths. "Thinking on one's feet" takes on added urgency when not doing so means that you starve.

As far as songwriting is concerned, nothing's changed. Those ancient hunting paths sound a lot like the so-called gig economy in which we are increasingly immersed. Musicians know this economy well—they *named it after us*—and instead of plugging into the imagination of the hunter-gatherer, we plug into the imagination of the hunter-creator. We get songs instead of carcasses. We drag them home and present them to our community. Hopefully, they eat.

Bonus Finding #1

Researchers noted that subjects who were walking gave *more total responses*, of *any* quality. They attributed this to the fact that walkers were simply more talkative in general and not necessarily "better" at the experiment. But it wasn't just blather: By generating ideas out loud, subjects were "iterating to find the deep structure of the prompt." In other words, Oppezzo and Schwartz backed into corroborating evidence that *quantity begets quality*. Fine, I'll say it: *They proved it!*

Bonus Finding #2

Tests focusing on convergent thinking had to come after the divergent tests because subjects became "demoralized" by the former. If you've ever engaged in a convergent task, like, oh, editing a song draft, you may have felt this yourself. Editing is a completely different skill. It navigates all kinds of constraints (rhyme, meter, melody, song form, and so on). If the divergent task is the hunt for ideas, convergent editing is about interpreting the carcass: *Edible? Which parts?*

In Defense of Convergent Thinking

Unfortunately, convergent tasks, like editing, separate early song drafts from their musical darlings, and the divergent side of us hates that. This internal tension, noted in the walking tests, spills out into external conflict between writers and editors or producers who embody each camp. The nightmare for convergent thinking is that, if it's doing its job right, it (1) is invisible and (2) makes our divergent tendencies look like the wellspring of all genius.

I've got to step in for convergent thinking for a second. Working with constraints is not demoralizing! It's awesome! To me, the only thing as exciting as that first flood of inspiration is the rush of "solving" it. I love clearing away *what it might be* and revealing *what it is*.

In class, I try to be as "kindly convergent" as possible. Even so, when I suggest cutting a section or swapping out a line, I'll watch student's faces flush and hear their voices waver with adrenaline. But I might also detect a twinge of anxiety, as if they just got caught trying to sell me a car with iffy brakes. And I understand: no one wants a demoralizing confrontation with the convergent mindset. Why? Ego, sure. Exhaustion, totally possible. Disappointment? Ha! That one's a given. James Baldwin has a great line about books, but you can substitute the word "song": "You never get the book you wanted, you settle for the book you get."

Rather than engage with convergence, divergent-leaning students will explode with a million ideas and then try to hide in plain sight among endless, flattening murk. To them I say: Resist the murk! Not every part of the carcass is edible! And if you're dead set on being murky, be clear about it! Be inscrutable! Precarious! Enigmatic! Elliptical! Oblong!(?) But please don't sell anybody a car with iffy brakes.

Digital Divergence

Digital audio workstations (or DAWs) make capture (divergent hunting) much easier, but they also give convergent editing a much bigger job. This is the downside to endless track space and horizonless time lines. In a session, you can pack song ideas on top of one another and defer all decisions until you're so lost in parts and bridges and marginalia that the seed of the song drowns in its own potential.

What some writers and producers do is re-create the limitations from earlier technologies. This means, yes, you have an infinite number of tracks, but *you only get to use four*. You can add as many effects as your processor can handle, but you *must* print them, meaning you have to choose on the spot, and the change can't be taken back. People work well with parameters, and when we don't have them, sometimes it helps to make them ourselves.

Convergence: The Rebrand

You know who deals with constraints all the time? Inventors. Engineers. Architects. Chefs. *Everyone*. Part of the appeal of Frank Gehry's free-form buildings is that they look like they have broken free from the rules. But that's a lie. Gehry did not solve gravity. The rules he addresses are the same rules that are in place for Folsom Prison, the pyramids, and your last snow fort.

My point: Don't hate the constraints, and lay off the constrainers. Thank them both. They provide opportunities for invention. Embrace the beleaguered convergent-thinking brain. It's our friend. And consider: Editors aren't baby murderers. *They're applied divergent thinkers.* They're guides. They're seers who survey the work from a different altitude. They're shamans who lead you to meaning. They're waiting, at the end of your walk, to carve up the carcass and make it a meal.

Practicing Convergence

How do we balance our divergent and convergent tendencies? I tell students to practice by *finishing songs as much as possible*. With a finished song, you present both your divergent vision and your convergent opinion. Put yourself in a hungry listener's shoes: Are they hoping for a carcass? Or a meal?

This is why starting a song is "easy" and finishing a song is "hard." But there's only one way to go pro. Be a finisher. Make it a meal.

Interlude: Five Gems from the Melodic Math Department

Melodic math is an approach to songwriting that stresses symmetry and prioritizes the melody. It's attributed to Max Martin, one of the most successful songwriters in pop music history, but the use of mathematical concepts in art predates him—by a lot. For instance, in 1712, German mathematician Gottfried Wilhelm Leibniz wrote, "Music is a secret exercise of arithmetic where the mind is unaware that it is counting. . . . [E]ven if the soul does not realize it is counting, it nevertheless feels . . . the pleasure in consonances or the vexation in dissonances." In other words, the listener can feel melodic math without knowing what it is. And that means it's an important tool for us to have in the kit.

If you're stuck in a revision, ask yourself some melodic math questions and see if they knock any answers loose. We've gone over some of these already, but here's a slightly different angle of approach.

1. Does the Melody Have Priority Over Everything Else?

If you play someone a song, then ask them to describe how the song went, what will they sing? Almost always, it'll be the melody, especially if it's been repeated. This means we need to have a melody that's worth repeating. Do you? If not, there's your primary place to revise.

One problem with your melody could be that you feel you have a great lyric, and you've let it dictate where the melody goes. In melodic math, *nothing* gets in the way of a good melody. Try revising by dropping the lyric, singing over whatever nonsense syllables come to mind, and then finding a lyric that will satisfy the sounds of those syllables. (David Byrne called this "emergent storytelling" earlier, if you recall.) It's not necessary for the resulting lyric to "make sense," but even the biggest melodic mathematicians know that "meaning" can be a powerful hook, too. When a listener discovers a lyric that translates a private experience into words they couldn't find on their own, that listener becomes a repeat listener and a potential fan for life. In a perfect world, both melody and lyric will be working toward that same goal.

2. Once You've Established a Melody, Do You Repeat It Strictly?

You are teaching a melody and planting a hook, so once you get an idea, let it sink in by *repeating it without straying*. Don't add a few syllables as a "pickup" to the repeated phrase. Don't vary the melodic shape. Don't give us a wicked vocal ad lib—that's like saying $2 + 2 = 4$ and then reestablishing it by saying $2 + 2 = 1 + 1 + \frac{1}{2} + \frac{1}{2} + \frac{1}{4} + \frac{1}{4} + \frac{1}{4} + \frac{1}{4}$. In melodic math, those are not equivalent. Find your melody, then mirror it.

Strict repetition is so important that, in some cases, the melody in the verse is exactly the same as the melody in the chorus. Boredom is avoided by singing different lyrics and building an arrangement that casts the repeated melody in a different light (re-harmonization, dynamic contrast, new instrumentation). The effect on the listener is that the first chorus sounds as if they've already heard it . . . *because they have.* Is that "lazy?" No. It's knowing what the brain likes (repetition), and delivering it in a way the brain likes (variation).

3. Are You Introducing Musical Ideas in an Orderly and Balanced Fashion?

Every few bars, introduce an element to draw the listener in without inundating them. Not too many parts at a time, and not too many parts in total, either—a song might have four to five, so no one gets overwhelmed. Overwhelmed people tend to skip to the next track.

To keep the song balanced, take a look at it from a higher altitude: If one section has a lot of words and melodic subdivisions, let the next section breathe with fewer words and longer phrases. "Sweet and salt" is how Max Martin put it in one of his (few) interviews.

4. Are Section Melodies Beginning in Different Places Relative to "the One"?

To be clear, "the one" is the first beat of the measure that starts a section. Eric Bazilian brought this up in his discussion of "Riff du Jour," but to break it down:

- Melodies that begin *after the one* feel conversational.
- Melodies *on the one* feel authoritative.
- Melodies that begin *before the one* feel urgent.

One rule of thumb is that a more conversational verse melody might start after the one, and a more urgent chorus melody will come in a few beats ahead of it. Try it. This little calculation can alter the entire flow of the song. (When a student brings in a draft that feels "stiff," this is one of the first places I check.)

5. Does the Chorus Contain Notes We Haven't Heard Yet?

They don't have to be the highest notes, but if they're new, they will differentiate the chorus from the other sections. Combined with repetition, these new sounds will spotlight the central melodic intent of the song. Try saving some money notes for the chorus, and then let them fly.

And it might go without saying, but make the chorus happen early. Sometimes I have A&R people come into class to listen to students' songs "like a real A&R person would," and if the chorus doesn't arrive within the first forty-five seconds or so, they hit Stop and then look at *me* like, "What the hell are you teaching these people?" It's awkward. Ways to avoid that:

- Start with the chorus.
- Start with an element of the chorus without giving it all away. Instead of singing the chorus melody, tease it on an instrument. If the listener feels teased, they're more likely to stick around.

200 Music, Lyrics, and Life

- Keep every section compact enough that the chorus lands before the A&R person starts reaching for the spacebar.

It's important to remember that melodic math is a tool, not a magic wand—you can follow it to the letter and still end up with garbage. Inspired ideas, like batteries, are not included. That said, I hope a few of these help you write yourself out of a jam, and into something that is uniquely yours.

Twenty

TRANSFORMATION COST

Remember: The rules, like streets, can only take you to known places. Underneath the grid is a field—it was always there—where to be lost is never to be wrong, but simply more.
—Ocean Vuong, *On Earth We're Briefly Gorgeous*

Revision's joys are private, and maybe that's why writing feels so solitary. If we do it right, no one can tell what caused the writing to happen. It's like we found it all under some mossy rock in Middle-earth. Good. They *shouldn't* know. We have the pages and pages of journals that yielded the crumbs of an idea, a lyric, a title spread over thousands of words and months of entries. There are verses still reaching out, blinking, asking where the hell they want to go, what they are trying to say. There's a first draft—complete garbage. Total embarrassment. Second draft, fifth draft, tenth draft. Even if we don't remember them specifically, they're in our bones—we can hear them when our spines crack as we rise from the desk.

I have folders full of past drafts; I loved a lot of them. They remind me of people whose phone numbers I used to know by heart. I knew what was in their fridge before opening the door, and I could have cooked in their kitchens blindfolded if they'd asked me to. I knew how their parents met, what they wanted to be when they grew up.

Fast-forward a couple years, and I don't know if they still live in the same city or if their parents are even alive. In some cases, our relationships exploded apart, and in others, one of us just slipped out the back door, French good-bye style, and *poof*, life got revised.

An immature part of me still wants to round all those people-memories up and yell, "No big loss!" but it's not always true. I miss some people until the pang of loss has melted into something I can't distinguish from physical pain. I carry them everywhere, there's no choice—we all walk with a limp, eventually—but sometimes loss is the cost of transformation.

Robert Frost said that he chose between one of two pretty much equal roads and that one day *he would say that his choice made all the difference*. He did *not* say that the roads had different values. He just took one because he couldn't take two. Did it make all the difference? How the hell would he know? He only took one. For all he knows, the two trails do what so many trails in the woods do—they split around some big old rock or fallen tree and merge back together fifty feet down the trail. To me, that poem is about marketing random choices and then selling the cost of transformation as clairvoyance. *I knew it all along.*

And poor Dorothy. Instead of having no facts, she gets bad facts. She lands in Oz, asks for directions out of town, starts walking, then finds out that the yellow brick road hits an unmarked(!) intersection. There she is, alone in the high corn, with a scarecrow hanging, semi-crucified, on a stand, realizing that "following the yellow brick road" does *not* yield her destination. None of them—from the mayor of Munchkin Land to the Lollipop Guild—have a clue how to get to Emerald City. But instead of shutting up and admitting it, the whole town breaks into a dance number essentially celebrating their ignorance. Dorothy buys the choreography because, wow, what a catchy melody, what simple directions, what *marketing*.

Dorothy, like Frost, blindly chooses a direction and lucks out. Nothing is made of this in the film.

The cost of Dorothy's transformation is the loss of her colorful new friends, and we all cry at this part because they're such great dancers, of course, but also because they are metaphors for difficult choices we, like Dorothy, have to make. But in swoops Hollywood to snatch joy from the mouth of tragedy, and a miracle occurs: *It was all a dream.* After clicking her heels and opening her eyes, Dorothy sees her old buddies at her bedside (". . . and you . . . and you were there . . ."), and we are left believing that, you know? You *can* gain without losing. Dreams really *do* come true.

Forget that choosing to dump people to get someplace better, then *finding the same people in that "better" place*, is actually a definition of hell.

What Dorothy learns instead is that *a perfect world is simply a place where one can choose without consequences.* Under her concussion-dampening washcloth, she enters a Kansas of the mind, where Transformation Cost does not exist. No wonder we love the movie—it allows us to travel over the rainbow without risking anything. We even get to keep the sentient lapdog that cheats death over and over again. Who doesn't wish their dog was immortal?

But the thing is: *There is no transformation without cost.* Revision has great benefits—our songs, they've gotten so much better! And yet, to get that benefit, we've had to kill our darlings, and now there are dead darlings everywhere. Some darlings are still crying out, "There's been a mistake! Save me! Don't you remember how we laughed when we first met? How you practiced your Grammy speech in the bathroom mirror? That was going to be *us.*"

Transformation Cost can haunt you if you let it. Those other yellow brick roads that fan out from the yellow brick intersection: Where did they go? Where are all the scarecrows of your other potential lives? Wasn't there a *red* brick road that spiraled out of town alongside the yellow? Is there somewhere *else* over the rainbow? Is it better there? What songs were sacrificed for the one you have? What will you never know for knowing what you do? *And what's it going to take to find an honest Munchkin in this town?*

Hey, so you're lost, eh? Okay. I see you've just committed murder and you want out of town. I get it.

So. Emerald City. Right. The Wizard—good guy, a little sketchy at times, but maybe you'll get him on a good day. You killed the right witch, if you know what I mean. So, that was lucky. Or instinctive?

Right, Emerald City. Sorry. Getting to that. Well, this is the road out of town, pretty clearly marked, just—well—that's a start, anyway. After that, I'm not sure. Never taken the trip, myself. But yeah, this is the first part, anyway, and from there you're kinda on your own. Might want to be mindful in some parts, I've heard stories, though frankly I've never been there, either. In fact, I've never been anywhere. I've been staring at that spiraling road out of town my whole Munchkin life and have no idea where it goes. Someday I'll be right here, among my own people, with kids and a steady job gilding lollipops, and I'll say that staying put and not taking that road out of town? Has made all the difference.

Twenty-One

FACING DOWN THE SECOND DRAFT

It's easy for me to say that revision is where pros and amateurs part company, but I thought it'd be important to give a real-world example that I was positive we both knew. The problem is that I have no idea what we have in common—except this book you're staring at. In whatever form you're staring at it. In whatever year it is. The fact that you're reading it means I must have done something right. But—and here's the point—I did *not* get it right on the first try. There were many, many demos.

I always wanted to write a book. I've written zines and sold them at shows for years. They're full of lyrics, and rants, and poems with big John Cage-y gaps between the words; on the early ones, I'd cut out the Oprah's Book Club approval stamp from somewhere and tape it on the cover. The zines always wanted to grow into something larger.

My first book attempt was based on a chart my dad created called "The Boxes." It was basically a logic tree that mapped out the step-wise path to one's life goals. My sisters and I used to do these instead of New Year's resolutions. Toward the end of the book, I realize that I don't fit in a box, or something. Honestly, I forget.

It was a terrible book.

I sent an early draft of it to MacDowell, an artists' residency in New Hampshire where geniuses go to finish their contributions to the literary canon. Isn't that what you're supposed to do? I didn't know. I remember someone on Facebook posting that he got in and was given the room where James Baldwin wrote part of *Notes of a Native Son*. I heard the kitchen dispatches silent deputies who tiptoe up to your door with baskets of croissants in the morning. No knocking—they wouldn't want to disturb your canon-altering work.

In my application to MacDowell, I included a promotional T-shirt and CD along with the book draft, as if it were a college radio station. You know, not a bribe, per se. Sometimes I wonder what became of the shirt. I know what became of the book. It's down here in the basement somewhere, which is where I am right now.

So, I wrote another book and stuck scrawled-on Post-it notes all over one of the basement walls. It was another terrible book. In one scene, I meet the ghost of my opera-singing, Italian immigrant grandmother in the parking lot of an Olive Garden. She blocks my way and demands that I explain how I would *dare* set foot in one. The Post-its eventually lost their stickiness and started falling off the wall, vacating their place in the book's alleged "time line." I usually write in silence, and when the Post-its fell, they'd startle me, as if they were New York City roaches, so big that I could hear their footsteps. Nope. Just my book, falling off the wall again.

Life continued, and over the years, I evolved from playing colleges to teaching at them, with concert tours thrown in during vacation time. Afraid that this might signal the end of my music career, I researched the source of the line, "Those who can, do; those who can't, teach," and it turns out, it's said by a character who's being a jerk in George Bernard Shaw's *Man and Superman*. I began studying Shaw's life because who the hell would have come up with crap like that? I cold-called actual Shaw scholars and took them out for coffee; I watched grainy videos of Shaw hanging around with Albert Einstein, who—guess what—was a professor. Sorry, but Einstein was a well-known doer, and apparently, Shaw did walk that line back a bit, not that anyone today would know. For reassurance, I looked up

"Doers who also teach," and the list is endless and humbling. I recommend you do the same.

One Shaw expert explained that English schools in Shaw's time were draconian propaganda machines intended to bolster the views of a waning empire. He drew lines to Beatles lyrics ("I used to get mad at my school / The teachers who taught me weren't cool"), Smiths lyrics ("Belligerent ghouls / Run Manchester schools"), Pink Floyd ("Hey! Teachers! Leave them kids alone!"), and Radiohead ("Bastard headmaster / I'm not going back"). Another scholar explained that the bad attitude toward teaching persists as the result of the "feminization of education"—the idea that, as more and more women became teachers, the opinion of the profession dropped.

I also learned about the Shaw Festival, an annual event in a town in Ontario, Canada. And I started another book—I'd go to the festival and do an investigative journalistic exposé like Bill Buford's *Among the Thugs*, but instead of exposing desperate, violent soccer hooligans, I'd uncover the seamy underside of Canadian theater festivalgoers.

Terrible.

Meanwhile, I fell in love with all of my students and, in particular, with a class I taught at Wesleyan. They were complete nut jobs—they showed up in 3-D glasses and wrote songs about getting hit by cars and flying through the air. After discovering that I was just an adjunct professor and couldn't guarantee my return, they asked if they could take my syllabus and petition the school so they could continue teaching it themselves. Wesleyan agreed, and in the same way artists cover other people's songs, my former students covered my class. I watched as something I'd made took on a life of its own.

And I started another book, about a "fictitious school" in the Connecticut woods—Brooks University—because why not. I guess you could have called it semi-fictional? Or just call it what it was:

Terrible.

But then, a new idea, and another book. Here's the elevator pitch: "How I learned what I teach, and teach what I've learned." In one chapter, I'd go to a class and give a solid piece of advice, and in the next chapter I'd flash back to me, on the road, screwing up hilariously and learning the exact class lesson the hard way. The ideas dragged me out of bed at 5 a.m.; I programmed the coffee machine to be ready and brewed, like an idling Batmobile.

This was going to be the one. I went through all of the exercises I've outlined in this book you're reading. I defined success. I made a "playlist" of great books, which book people call a Competitive Analysis. I also took a book—Zadie Smith's *Swing Time*—and charted it out, the way I do with songs in class. I figured this might be something one would do in writing grad school or in James Baldwin's room at MacDowell. I picked *Swing Time* because it has two time lines working in tandem, and some of it was pop music–based, with a character that kind of reminded me of Madonna. Fish in a barrel, right? *Fish in a barrel.*

I finished a bunch of chapters, went to Staples and bought all the paper, then fed it through my printer. The pages flowed into the catch tray like Grecian silk billowing from the loom. Like a million covers of the *Daily Gazette* unspooling from the printing press, all of their front pages reading WAR IS OVER . . . WAR IS OVER . . . WAR IS OVER . . .

Before going to agents with my chapters (I'd read a book on writing books, and that's what you do next), I was able to get it read by "someone in the industry." I waited an excruciating week for feedback. Picture a lumbering man about the size of an ex–first baseman, nonchalantly ordering a cup of coffee at a bodega, only he's completely on fire. That was me.

The feedback arrived. It wasn't terrible, exactly. It was half terrible. *Which means it was half good.* They thought the chapters were promising, fun, and insightful, but the problem was that there were two stories kind woven into each other (which was the whole idea). The result, they felt, was confusion.

The fire went out, and charred-me stopped waking up early. I quit writing, *forever*. I told my wife she was free to go, just leave if she wanted, no questions asked. "I'd leave me, too," I told her. I started apologizing to everyone. My parents asked, "For what?" "Oh. Everything."

I dragged myself into class, having no idea why anyone would listen to me or if I should quit that, too, to staunch the flow of fraudulence leaking from me. And then I began getting a stream of emails from MacDowell about Pulitzer-winning alums gathering for their annual "celebration of the paragraph," or whatever. They'd put me on their mailing list.

But then, I started writing again. I guess I just enjoy it more than it hurts?

You may be writing a song right now and asking yourself if you enjoy it more than it hurts, which is why I'm telling you all this to begin with. We're all connected. We're all going through it. I've released enough records to know that the release is a blip compared to the Basement Days of putting it together. I'm with you, and I feel for you, and you may be more bruised and battered than I'll ever understand, but if you're compelled, you're going to stay on the horse. I hope you do.

Twenty-Two

IS IT DONE?

This is a popular question: *How do I know when the song is finished?*

I think it's related to how we know when a party's over: It's when we've seen everyone we'd hoped to see; when the food's gone and the good bottles are empty; when the talk starts getting both louder and dumber; when we become aware that we're guests; and when spidey sense tells us that we're sticking around for selfish reasons.

An old salt bandleader gave me a piece of advice I've never forgotten: Leave the party early.

Things Must End

Our finished songs get recorded, and they go on to live a life of their own.

But what happens to all our unfinished songs? All the false starts and mumbled melodies waiting for lyrics? All those doors, knocked on and walked away from, unopened?

They're alive. And like a program running in the background of your computer, they're draining energy.

In the 1920s, Lithuanian-Soviet psychologist Bluma Zeigarnik conducted a study around waiters who could remember complicated orders, but were no longer able to recall details of the transaction soon after the bill was paid. She concluded that unfinished tasks continue actively working on the mind and are remembered more clearly than finished ones. Her assertions, published in 1927's "On Finished and Unfinished Tasks," have come to be known as the Zeigarnik effect.

Here's a super-scientific example: In the movie *Who Framed Roger Rabbit*, the evil Judge Doom searches for the cartoon bunny Roger by tapping out the first part of "Shave and a Haircut," knowing Roger can't handle leaving it unfinished. ("No toon can resist the old 'Shave and a Haircut' trick.") Behind a speakeasy wall, Roger begins convulsing at the lack of musical resolution until it drives him mad and he bursts through the wall, singing, ". . . *Two bits!*"

The brain is a nag that can't rest when there's unfinished business. We might not crash through walls, but we do get anxious when we have "too much on our plate" or a thousand browser tabs open. We hate when shows promise "To Be Continued" and then get canceled. We let unrequited love affairs spiral into a fantasyland of "if only," whereas a relationship that has run its course can, for better or worse, resolve. Incompleteness creates clutter, and unfinished songs add to the pile.

Things Must End

Thanks to social media, I'm in touch with people from grammar school, from the summer camp I got thrown out of for drinking in the woods, from my first record label, from my second record label, from the defunct magazine where I used to work. I know what my high school biology lab partner has to say about Beyoncé, or grilled salmon, or Mondays. Last time I saw her, we were gutting a frog.

Things Must End

I'm Facebook friends with my old hometown. Not the Chamber of Commerce, or a tourism board (as if)—the *town*. I moved away eons ago; all that's left that I'd recognize are the graveyards and a liquor store with undersized shopping carts that made me sad. But now? I'm up to the minute on water main breaks, and the library's new parking lot, and . . .

Things Must End

Forgetting is one way we burn the crops to make room for new growth, but the past can step out of the flames and un-end itself.

Things Must End

Some of us should be dead to each other, not in the bad way, just in the "make room" way.

Make It Stop

The most important thing we can do is finish.

The second most important thing we can do is start the next song immediately.

The third most important thing we can do is keep our files organized so we can start and finish in a frictionless environment.

Finished songs have a future among the living. Unfinished songs drag chains across the attic floor, slam the cabinetry, flick on the stove, and startle the dog. They're tortured souls seeking rest; phantom singles on unrequited records.

Finish because it's begging you. Finish because you don't know what it is. Finish to clear space for new versions of "Shave and a Haircut."

Two bits!

New Tool Alert: Experience

The act of finishing songs makes the *feeling* of finishing more familiar. Quantity begets quality, partly because quantity also begets *experience*. This is how our heroes did it—they did it by *doing it*. This means getting ready—excited!—for a ton of failure. Because there's good news: experience is failure's parting gift. "Here. This is for next time." *Take the gift.*

The guests I spoke with throughout this book have failed a *lot*, and each lesson refined their series of choices. Really, the most important thing you can mimic is their number of attempts and their ability to pull elegant solutions out of a hot, stinking bag of failure.

Experience Leaves a Trail

Our repeated solutions form a pattern over time, and that pattern becomes recognizable; our approach becomes our "style."

Susan Sontag writes, "Every style is a means of insisting on something." Here's a prompt for your journal: If style is a means of insisting on something, *what is it you insist on?*

Clues That You Might Be Finished

1. **No more itches.** If your bridge is a throwaway or your chorus isn't paying off, it will not magically pay off down the road. You know where it itches. Scratch it until no more scratching is required.
2. **No disclaimers.** There's such a joy—and a power—in feeling like you don't have to set a song up or adjust the expectations of the listener. Instead of pointing out itches or flaws before

your song plays, recite the following: "Just hit Play. I hope you're wearing a helmet. And a diaper. Why? Because the song is *that good*."

That's "finished" energy.

3. **Hydroplaning.** Toward the end of every semester, revised songs begin to deliver—and lighten—like boats that get up to speed and begin skimming the waves instead of plowing through them. In these moments, I forget what I'm supposed to be doing, which is teaching, and just start listening. It stops being songwriting class, and the song stops being music; it becomes a transporting experience. It's not "the perfect song" that does it, either—it's the one that feels connected to the artist's intent.

4. **The mix is deliberate.** People who are not confident in a song find a thousand ways to overcompensate elsewhere. They pull the lead vocal back and wash the whole track in reverb and synths and ambience and *everything but the song*. For some, an unfocused mix is an aesthetic choice, sure. For some, the lyrics are just impressions and are not intended to be ruminated on or even understood. But I've found that the majority of songs that try to bury themselves inside themselves do so because they are not yet confident in what they are.

Conversely, nothing is more exciting than when a revision comes back into class and the lead vocal has been nudged *up* in the mix; the choices, even if murky, are intentionally so. Everything becomes stronger and more confident, including the singer, who's now actually saying something they believe in, and the *writer*, who lives outside the song, presenting a polished, focused thought.

5. **The writer disappears.**

> "I believe it was John Cage who told me, 'When you start working, everybody is in your studio—the past, your friends, enemies, the art world, and above all, your own ideas—all are there. But as you continue painting, they start leaving, one by one, and you are left completely alone. Then, if you are lucky, even you leave.'"—Philip Guston

When a song leaves the listener with their own reflection, and not the writer's, it feels attached to something larger than where it came from. The song doesn't feel like it came *from* anyone; it feels like it's been here all along.

6. **Time and space bend.** Some songs have the ability to loosen the logic constraints they're under. We think, "How could that have been only 2:30? I was a million miles away . . ." or "How does that song feel so massive? It's just piano and voice . . ." After a while, what seems like a weird quirk of the art form starts becoming an indicator that the art is working.

   The premise of Mark Danielewski's novel *House of Leaves* is that a family's house, when measured, is somehow bigger on the inside than it is on the outside. Improbable for an architect, a screw-up for a surveyor, but it's actually what a songwriter shoots for. In music, the impossible happens all the time.

7. **You wind up back at the beginning.** This is the moment we stop asking if our bridge is too short or long and instead start wondering if we've done our listeners the service we are entrusted with.

   Did we say what we came to say?

Accidental Endings Are Endings, Too

I love the idea that someone might start a song and know that the finished product is going to be a song. The leap in logic there is surreal and not backed by history—experience teaches us a different lesson.

Example: Hennig Brand was a seventeenth-century German alchemist who went on a quest for the "philosopher's stone," the substance that would turn metal into gold. One of the ingredients he required for this transformation was human urine. Lots of it. Over one two-week period, he boiled down around 1,200 gallons of urine, distilled it, and guess what did *not* come out? Gold. Guess what *did* come out? A waxy, glowing lump that easily burst into flames. He combined the Greek "phos" (light) with "phorous" (bearer), and so phosphorous was named. Disgusting? Yes. The point? You never know what you're going to find once you start looking.

Hennig Brand did not fail—he just succeeded at something else. There are so many stories like Hennig Brand's; why should yours be any different? Half the things we use on a daily basis were discovered while looking for something else. A lot of things we write were intended to be something else, too.

Twenty-Three

NO, REALLY: WHEN IS IT DONE?

asked the same basic question to each of the people I interviewed for this book. Here are some highlights:

How do you know when a song is done?

Madison Emiko Love: I feel like I just know. It's also a good sign when my publisher tells me, "It's fire, the artist loves it and doesn't want to change anything." I'm always willing to write and rewrite songs until the artist is happy, but honestly, the day I write a song, if that's how I'm feeling in the second verse, that's probably how it's going to be when you hear it on the radio.

How do you know when a painting is done?

John Currin: Oh God. Uh . . . it's just hard to answer. Part of the struggle of being an artist is that question right there because you know, everybody overdoes things. Like, you know that feeling when there's a song where they can't help but put in strings and it's just, *Goddammit. Why did you put the strings in?* I was driving in Maine and a song came on—Terry Jacks's "Seasons in the Sun." "We had joy, we had fun, we had seasons in the sun . . ." And it has a really affecting and strange down-tuned guitar or whatever they use in the beginning—really kind of a menacing, cool sound. And then the song starts, and it's pretty sparse, right? It's that guy with his little boy's voice and everything, and then when they go to the second verse they bring in *strings*, you know, and it's just, *Fuck you. Why did you do that? We already know it's a super sad song.* And that's a thing with paintings. Sometimes I think, *You know what, don't bring the strings in.*

How do you know when a song is done?

Eric Bazilian: That's a great question. Sometimes they aren't ever. I'd say one rule of thumb is that the quicker and more "inspired"—literally, "breathed in"—a song is, the more likely it's finished by first draft.

How do you know when a tire is done?

Jennifer Basl: Performance targets for a given product are set based on the intended market for that product. Once we have a design that meets or exceeds those targets, then it goes to production.

How do you know when an improv sketch is done?

Phil LaMarr: My friend used to say, "Improv is the toilet paper of theater. No matter how brilliant you are, you just tear off that sheet and move on to the next."

How do you know when a story is done?

George Saunders: Um, that's actually the million-dollar question for anybody. For me, as I'm editing over the course of my story, my standards keep going up. So, I often think a story is done one month in, and then suddenly, one part of it will just . . . get better. And then you look at the rest of the story, in relation to that part, and go, "Oh, not done." And then you keep revising those other parts up. What'll usually happen is a certain section of text will get into a state where I can't see anything to change about it. Or, a better way to say it is, it's producing little thrills that I recognize as high-level thrills that I don't want to give away. So therefore it's staying.

By then, we're in a very elevated zone . . . the reader and I are speaking a very high-level poetry back and forth. You can get away with a lot of omission. We both know what questions are on the table, what bowling pins are in the air. But basically: I run out of stuff to revise. The whole story becomes what I think of as "undeniable." And usually there's just a few paragraphs and then a few lines at the end that need revising. And whatever remaining questions are going to get answered in there. Learning to ride out that editing process until the very end is one thing I've learned over the years. But the short answer is, it's a feeling. And I suppose learning to recognize that "this is finished" feeling is what any artist is working toward.

Twenty-Four

DEALING WITH CRITICS

There's a 100 percent chance that not everyone will love your work. It's inevitable, and it sucks. What can I tell you? Sticking your neck out is brave, and knives are cheap.

Some people will tell you, "Don't read reviews. They're warping when they're bad, and they're warping when they're good." If that works for you, great, but personally, I've noticed that fake-ignoring things only mythologizes them. Sometimes you just have to open the door and deal with whatever's in there.

Example: I had a girlfriend who turned into a semi-stalker. It got kind of scary. Weeks after we broke up, I got phone calls from somewhere on my block telling me that I looked so good walking into my apartment building. I'd inch my way over to my eighth-floor window and scan the pedestrians and dog walkers, looking for her holding a phone to her ear and waving. I'd check both directions before stepping out into the hallway of my building. I don't know what I was expecting.

My inbox filled with emails from her with long, breathless bricks of text. I didn't block her address because I didn't want her to sense that I was reacting. I figured that if I just waited it out, the dissatisfaction would bore her enough to move on. It's the same kind of thing you're supposed to do in the wild if confronted by a bear.

I was scared of what might be in those emails, and tortured myself by guessing at the contents: wild bolts of desperation, anger, jealousy, insanity. Violence? Maybe there were threats. I researched restraining orders and what I was legally allowed to do in self-defense. I archived her emails as evidence in case I was found murdered, and they sat in my hard drive, unread, gnawing at me. When I couldn't take it anymore, I gathered my courage and opened the one sitting fresh in my inbox.

She opened by talking about her day: the sun rising up from the row of apartments out the window of her Brooklyn bedroom, the morning stretching out with the promise of new adventures, the joy with which she lives her life, her gratitude for all that she has—the health, the goodwill, the people. Speaking of people, she got around to how sad it was that our relationship had "hit a snag," how things were all so different now, how I would understand this if I only had the capacity to empathize, to be emotionally flexible—she hoped that someday I'd be able to see my way around my self-imposed obstacles.

She was giving me a bad review.

She talked about the world of people I was missing as they grew up: nieces and nephews I'd met at family functions, best friends, parents, all with luxurious, enviable lives—lives so full of *life*, you know?—and how I was missing it all. Wasn't it sad? Wasn't I really the one wasting his life? Wasn't I, all along, the problem?

It went on like this for longer than I will ever know because I read until I found myself getting really bored—the *last* reaction I'd prepared for. I went to the folder I'd named "Evidence" and scanned a few more. No threats, no violence, no power, just a dump of poorly considered, passive-aggressive, but ultimately tiresome thoughts. A digital trove of bad reviews.

The emails contained what I now refer to as the Plague of Universal Tedium. They were words intended as communication that, when strung together, accidentally translated into a description of the vacuum that exists between us all. As I dragged the Evidence folder to the trash, I wondered which is worse: that there could be a monster under my bed or that there never, *ever* is, and there never will be anything under there but dust and stray socks? I think it's a toss-up.

So, if trying to ignore reviews doesn't work and reading them is also painful, here's a corrective lens and an actionable plan: Read them, and stop reading the moment you contract the Plague of Universal Tedium. Hopefully, this will not take long because there are better uses for your time than staring into a circus mirror wondering if that's what you really look like.

Twenty-Five

MONEY

In a visit to my class, singer-songwriter Madison Cunningham advised, "Put your money where your art is, and take the pay cut." Would you take that deal?

Musicians and songwriters don't make a lot of money, on average. That has always been the case. To make it worse, there's an entire library of music jokes waiting to ridicule you for not thinking about this before you chose how to spend your time. Let me ruin a few, if you haven't heard them yet:

What do you call a drummer without a girlfriend? Homeless.
What did St. Peter say to the bassist at the Pearly Gates? You can load in through the kitchen.
What's the difference between a folk singer and a large pizza? A large pizza can feed a family of four.

I could go on.

The jokes are funny because something rings true. What is it? It's *how much we'll suffer through for music*. We love it. We'll do anything to keep writing and playing songs. (I was a temp at a New York ad agency for so long, they used to call me "Perm.") Half the internet was built on the backs of musicians who loved it enough to do it—and give it away—for free.

We dream in broad daylight, which is such a childlike thing to do, especially to so-called practical, serious-minded people. Hence, the classic:

> A boy says to his mom, "I'm going to grow up and be a musician." Mom smiles and says, "Son, you can't do both."

That is, unless you can.

Don't Worry About Getting Fired

We talked about money being one of those collaborators that doesn't make it to the credits. It can influence what you write, where your choruses land, where you place your title settings, how you choose your language, how you approach "blue" notes, and so on. In our conversations, Janna Levin (the cosmologist) and I got into the relationship between art and money. Here's her take on it.

> *In reading your work, I noticed a common theme running through music and astronomical research, which is that everyone is always worried about getting fired.*

Oh my God. Yeah.

> *So, my question—and this is often raised with the arts—is: Who is guiding the history of your field? To what degree is it the money and not the science?*

The money facilitates it, but it doesn't drive it. And if it does, then we're doing something really bad. *Really* bad. Totally foul. And it's always bad projects, always. The best projects are absolutely where the thought comes first. And *then* they decide, "This means so much to me and to science that I'm gonna fight like hell to get this money."

I realize you may feel like we're out on a limb here, but the analogies to the music industry are so obvious . . .

I *don't* think we're out on a limb because my husband's also a musician. This has been my life—like, *Where's the money? Where's the talent? Where's the art?*

And then people show up with tons of money to fund bad projects.

Like, you know, boy bands.

[Laughs] Sure.

Boy bands are the example. Sometimes boy bands pick somebody who's incredibly talented who goes on to be amazing as an individual. But the money comes first, and then the music. Those are very cynical projects.

I mean, money is a strange thing. Think about climbing Mount Everest—like, why would anyone *do* that? Why do you want to climb Mount Everest . . . and die? And it's because of this *desire to have a view from the summit.* And that's what physicists are doing. They're sacrificing their happiness, their monetary success—I mean, all of us could make a fucking mint if we went into "reality"—and we sacrifice it all for a glimpse from the summit. And we wanna come down the mountain and share it. Tell people about it. *Look at what I saw.*

And I tell this to my son all the time, you know, you just need enough to have a roof over your head, and the rest is *yours.* You know? *The rest is yours.* Strive for that. Strive for the minimum that you need to survive and be creative. If you acquire affluence, great—but that's not what you're going for. What you're going for is just enough to be able to create.

Twenty-Six

THE END OF THIS BOOK IS THE BEGINNING OF YOUR NEXT SONG

'm not really the "good-bye" type, and I'm not going to start now.
Instead, I will magically transform from an author back to a guy
who's a little farther down the road and who can point out some of
the potholes you might want to avoid. I'll be on whatever passes for
social media and will supplement the ideas you've read, so in a way
the book is only done if you want it to be.

Earlier, I said that some former students are doing well somewhere in the music industry. They're all doing different things, but I
found some patterns among them that may be interesting, inspiring,
or even just calming.

First: What Did They *Not* Have in Common?

1. **They all had different skill sets, and played different instruments at different levels of mastery with different styles of
   music.**
2. **They were interested in different parts of the industry.** They
   wanted to be in pop music, video games, virtual reality, Broadway, film scoring—they've become cantors, rappers, country
   singers, DJs, and divas who roll around on the floor in videos
   for songs they wrote in class.

3. **They were not more orthodox about form than anyone else.** Strict pop writers are doing well, and people writing stratospheric ambient "settings" are doing well. Some are not even writers anymore—they mix, remix, master, produce, promote, or protect, via copyright law or management, the music they love. One guy racked up millions of streams on Spotify based on forty seconds of a handheld recording of beach sounds.

4. **They were not necessarily more or less "artsy" than anyone else.** Crazy hair and outlandishness are not indicators of imagination, vision, or desire to create. Just as often in my class, it's the quiet, buttoned-up one who burns the room down with a new song.

5. **They were not necessarily doing *then* what they are doing *now*.** Some had an aesthetic together, but many others were searching for something that arrived years later. My favorite example of this is a student who came into my class as a self-proclaimed "lyricist" with no interest in the music part of things. Now? She's a world-class DJ living in Europe, pushing her own style of dance music, with not a lyric to be found. Maybe that will come as a comfort to those of you who are still searching, no matter where you are in your present creative arc.

6. **They were not necessarily the most talented.** Music is not a meritocracy. If it were, we'd more or less know how the story ends.

So, What *Did* They Have in Common?

1. They showed up to class on time, ready to roll, with a song, assignment, paper, whatever.

2. They were open to all forms of collaboration and to as many experiences as possible. These were the people whose names came up regularly when students presented a draft: "So I wrote

this with X . . . ," "I wrote it alone, but X jumped in on guitar . . . ," "This is for a project I'm launching with X . . ."—over and over. The person in your life who gets the question "When do you sleep?" is the one I'm talking about.

3. **They were all strong at journaling and getting their ideas down, whether it was on paper, or in their phone, or however they decided to do it.** They took writing seriously and prioritized it in their lives.

4. **They sought me out for office hours.** I can look at my past calendar and show you a list of people who are doing something cool in the industry now. That is *not* a reflection of me as someone who said anything magical but rather a reflection of their hunger to understand the craft and what more they could be doing.

5. **They all knew that this is a people industry and were generous to their peers when it came to comments, critique, and so on.** Through genuine curiosity about others' work, they began building a reputation and a network for themselves.

6. **They were all prepared for luck.** They worked really hard for a moment they were not promised and that may never have arrived, but they were ready when it did.

The Closer

Hopefully, I've helped you connect to the discipline we call "songwriting," but most of these connections apply to anything—and that's the point. It's an orientation to life. We just get to sing about it. Some of you probably feel like you're in murky places, writing-wise, to which I say congratulations for wrestling and writing through it. Stay patient: you may feel like the pieces add up to nothing, but you also may have tripped over a musical Rosetta Stone that'll inform your future work. I suspect it's a little of both.

Part of the job is to protect your growing voice, so shake off the haters, the eye rollers, and the non-believers. Take the ideas and the stories you found useful here, and follow your journal wherever it leads. Write your Mission Songs. Puncture-proof your tires. Fish your wild rivers. Sing your blues. Boil your urine. Rearrange your deck chairs. Say "no" to Elvis. Say "Yes, and . . ." to the universe.

Trust, and be trustworthy.

ACKNOWLEDGMENTS

Sally Law Errico, for everything

Cate and Michael, for braving the pandemic, the deadline, and the broccoli

Angela, Michael, Melanie, and Melissa

John Cerullo and Carol Flannery at Backbeat Books; Ed Grauer, Esq.; Carrie Howland; Mike Edison, an editor who knows why Charlie Watts matters

Early Readers

Syd Sidner, Barbara Jones, Kristen Schleifer, Lara Evans, Burkhard Bilger, and Alan Light

Guests

Paul Stanley, George Saunders, Phil LaMarr, John Currin, Janna Levin, Shane McAnally, Eric Bazilian, Madison Emiko Love, Eva Grace Hendricks, Jim Anderson, Jack Stratton, Jennifer Basl, Lee Dannay, David Pasquesi, Madison Cunningham, Nina Katchadourian, Raul Midón, Bob Donnelly, Ben Small, Matt Beck, Ben Mink, Greg Felt, "Anonymous A&R Person," Rob Thomas, and Benny Blanco

Enablers and Cosigners

Kevin Hicks, Hal Brooks, Jessica Helfand, Bronwen Hruska, Jake Schwartz, Kelly Corrigan, Ed Lichty, Evan Stanley, Andy Barzvi, Bill Washabaugh, John Devore, Adam Sternbergh, Amanda Petrusich, Ben Ratliff, Marat Berenstein, Matt Wang, David Schmittgens, Marc Plotkin, Jamie Siegel, David Staller, Kathleen Kennon, Stephen Brown-Fried, Dan Charnas, Greg Erickson, Ilene Donin, the good people at Books Are Magic, Bob McGrory, Laura Van Wie McGrory, Rebecca Lemov, Alex Schuh, Darin Strauss, Paul Giamatti, Maggie Rogers, Elyse Cheney, Jeb Brown, Tom Revelle, Nick Sansano, Al Coppola, Michael Blume, Paul Leo, Cyrus T. Elk, Ani Klang, Nick Cianci, Kate Yeager, Gabriella De La Cruz, Will Zesiger, Steph Butchko, Sofia D'Angelo, Julie Hanse, the choir on "Here's to the End of the World," Claire Hawkins, Kyle Duke, Jack Schneider, Chloe Gasparini, all Eclectics everywhere, Brett Castro, Madeline Boreham, Cameron Franklin, Hannah Gross, readers of *Tallboy* magazine (it's all your fault), Pete Ganbarg, Brian Reed, Vivek J. Tiwary, Hana Elion, JJ Mitchell, Khaya Cohen, Hans Bilger, Sarah Solovay, Molly Kirschenbaum, Ben Lapidus, Matt Nathanson, Bob Power, Tim Pattison, Joe D'Ambrosio, Josie Carrero, Machan Taylor, Linda Lorence-Critelli, Terry Tompkins, Jacob Slichter, Cynthia Kaplan, Brian Long, Molly Neuman, Jonatha Brooke, Stein Bjelland, Juliann Garey, Dan Freeman, Jonathan Bernstein, Susan Misner, Matt Morrissey, Kenny Gardner, the faculty and staff at New York University's Clive Davis Institute of Recorded Music, Yale University, and Wesleyan University.

And my students, who I root for every step of the way.

APPENDIX: SUMMER READING LIST FOR SOMETIME LATER IN LIFE

Here's a chunk of my bookshelf.

Each of these titles helped shape the thoughts in this book. There are more—oh God, so many more—but this list will hold you for a bit.

Abdurraqib, Hanif. *They Can't Kill Us until They Kill Us*

Azerrad, Michael. *Our Band Could Be Your Life*

Ball, David. *Backwards and Forwards: A Technical Manual for Reading Plays*

Brennan, Ian, and Tunde Adebimpe. *Silenced by Sound: The Music Meritocracy Myth*

Brookfield, Stephen D. *The Skillful Teacher: On Technique, Trust, and Responsiveness in the Classroom*

Bryson, Bill. *A Walk in the Woods: Rediscovering America on the Appalachian Trail*

Byrne, David. *How Music Works*

Cage, John. *Silence: Lectures and Writing,*

Cain, Susan. *Quiet: The Power of Introverts in a World That Can't Stop Talking*

Cameron, Julia. *The Artist's Way: A Spiritual Path to Higher Creativity*

Chee, Alexander. *How to Write an Autobiographical Novel*

Coates, Ta-Nehisi. *Between the World and Me*

DiFranco, Ani. *No Walls and the Recurring Dream: A Memoir*

Dillard, Annie. *The Writing Life*

Dyer, Geoff. *But Beautiful: A Book about Jazz*

Harari, Yuval Noah. *Sapiens: A Brief History of Humankind*

Hickey, Dave. *Air Guitar: Essays on Art and Democracy*

Hindman, Jessica Chiccehitto. *Sounds Like Titanic*

Hoagland, Tony, with Kay Cosgrove. *The Art of Voice: Poetic Principles and Practice*

Hyde, Lewis. *A Primer for Forgetting: Getting Past the Past*

Kagge, Erling. *Silence in the Age of Noise*

Karr, Mary. *The Art of Memoir*

King, Stephen. *On Writing: A Memoir of the Craft*

Klinkenborg, Verlyn. *Several Short Sentences About Writing*

Kurtz, Glenn. *Practicing*

Lamott, Anne. *Bird by Bird*

Lanier, Jaron. *Ten Arguments for Deleting Your Social Media Accounts Right Now*

Lanier, Jaron. *Who Owns the Future?*

Levin, Janna. *Black Hole Blues and Other Songs from Outer Space*

Light, Alan. *The Holy or the Broken: Leonard Cohen, Jeff Buckley and the Unlikely Ascent of "Hallelujah"*

Manson, Mark. *The Subtle Art of Not Giving a F*ck*

Martin, Steve. *Born Standing Up*

McPhee, John. *Draft No. 4: On the Writing Process*

Murakami, Haruki. *What I Talk About When I Talk About Running*

Nelson, Maggie. *Bluets*

Nunez, Sigrid. *The Friend*

Odell, Jenny. *How to Do Nothing: Resisting the Attention Economy*

Pattison, Pat. *Writing Better Lyrics*

Petrusich, Amanda. *Do Not Sell at Any Price: The Wild, Obsessive Hunt for the World's Rarest 78rpm Records*

Pirsig, Robert. *Zen and the Art of Motorcycle Maintenance: An Inquiry into Values*

Questlove, with Ben Greenman. *Creative Quest*

Ruefle, Mary. *Madness, Rack, and Honey: Collected Lectures*

Sagan, Carl. *Contact*

Saunders, George. *The Braindead Megaphone*

Smith, Patti. *Just Kids*

Smith, Zadie. *Swing Time*

Solnit, Rebecca. *A Field Guide to Getting Lost*

Thompson, Derek. *Hit Makers: How to Succeed in an Age of Distraction*

Tweedy, Jeff. *Let's Go (So We Can Get Back): A Memoir of Recording and Discording with Wilco, Etc.*

Vuong, Ocean. *On Earth We're Briefly Gorgeous*

Watts, Alan. *The Wisdom of Insecurity: A Message for an Age of Anxiety*

Yagoda, Ben. *The B-Side: The Death of Tin Pan Alley and the Rebirth of the Great American Song*

BIBLIOGRAPHY

Full-length interviews, related chapters, playlists, articles, and other gems are available at my website, www.errico.com. If further immersion is what you're looking for, I'd check there first—the people I spoke to are endlessly fascinating, whether or not I was able to include them here.

Abdurraqib, Hanif. *They Can't Kill Us until They Kill Us*. Columbus, OH: Two Dollar Radio, 2017.

Aguayo, Rafael. *Dr. Deming: The American Who Taught the Japanese about Quality*. New York: Fireside Books, 1990.

Amazon Staff. "Live from Las Vegas, it's re:MARS 2019." *Amazon*, June 2, 2019. https://www.aboutamazon.com/news/innovation/live-from-las-vegas-its-re-mars-2019

AnnaOutdoors. "10 Tips for Car Living." March 7, 2014. https://annaoutdoors.wordpress.com/2014/03/07/tips-for-living-out-of-a-car

Ball, David. *Backwards and Forwards: A Technical Manual for Reading Plays*. Carbondale: Southern Illinois University Press, 1983.

Benjamin, Walter. *Reflections: Essays, Aphorisms, Autobiographical Writings*. New York: Schocken Books, 1986.

Bergler, Edmund. "Does 'Writer's Block' Exist?" *American Imago* 7, no. 1 (1950): 43–54. http://www.jstor.org/stable/26301237

Bradbury, Ray. *Zen in the Art of Writing*. Santa Barbara, CA: Joshua Odell Editions, 1996.

Brennan, Ian, and Tunde Adebimpe. *Silenced by Sound: The Music Meritocracy Myth*. Oakland, CA: PM Press, 2019.

Brookfield, Stephen D. *The Skillful Teacher: On Technique, Trust, and Responsiveness in the Classroom*. San Francisco: Jossey-Bass, 2006.

Brooklyn Museum. Exhibit, "Hip-Hop Nation: Roots, Rhymes, and Rage," Brooklyn, New York, September 22, 2000–December 31, 2000. https://www.brooklynmuseum.org/opencollection/exhibitions/746

Brox, Jane. *Silence: A Social History of One of the Least Understood Elements of Our Lives*. New York: Houghton Mifflin Harcourt, 2019.

Bryson, Bill. *A Walk in the Woods: Rediscovering America on the Appalachian Trail*. New York: Broadway Books, 1998.

Buford, Bill. *Among the Thugs*. London: Secker & Warburg, 1990.

Byrne, David. *How Music Works*. New York: Three River Press, 2012.

Cadogan, Garnette. "Walking While Black." *LitHub*, July 8, 2016. https://lithub.com/walking-while-black

Cage, John. *Silence: Lectures and Writings*. Middletown, CT: Wesleyan University Press, 1961.

Cain, Susan. *Quiet: The Power of Introverts in a World That Can't Stop Talking*. New York: Broadway Books, 2012.

Cameron, Julia. *The Artist's Way: A Spiritual Path to Higher Creativity*. New York: Jeremy P. Tarcher/Putnam, 1992.

Caplan, Walker. "No, Beinecke Library Is Not Specially Designed to Suffocate Humans in the Event of a Fire." *LitHub*, February 16, 2021. https://lithub.com/no-beinecke-library-is-not-specially-designed-to-suffocate-humans-in-the-event-of-a-fire

Carey, John. *What Good Are the Arts?* New York: Oxford University Press, 2006.

Chaucer, Geoffrey. "The Complaint of Mars." In *The Works of Geoffrey Chaucer: The William Morris Kelmscott Chaucer*, 226–28. New York: Calla Editions, 2017.

Chee, Alexander. *How to Write an Autobiographical Novel*. New York: Mariner Books, 2018.

Collins, Chris. "A Texas Community Chokes on Fecal Dust from Cattle Feedlots." *Food and Environment Reporting Network*, February 3, 2020.

https://thefern.org/2020/02/a-texas-community-chokes-on-fecal-dust
-from-cattle-feedlots

Coolidge, Clark, ed. *Philip Guston: Collected Writings, Lectures, and Conversations.* Berkeley: University of California Press, 2011.

Cosmos. Season 1, episode 9, "The Lives of the Stars." Directed by Adrian Malone, David Kennard. Aired November 23, 1980. https://www.imdb.com/title/tt0760463

Dalí, Salvador. *50 Secrets of Magic Craftsmanship.* Translated by Haakon Chevalier. New York: Dial Press, 1948.

Danielewski, Mark Z. *House of Leaves.* New York: Pantheon Books, 2000.

DiFranco, Ani. *No Walls and the Recurring Dream: A Memoir.* New York: Viking, 2019.

Dillard, Annie. *The Writing Life.* New York: Harper Perennial, 1989.

Draney, James. "Are We Different Writers When We Move from Longhand to Screen?" *Lit Hub,* August 18, 2017. https://lithub.com/are-we
-different-writers-when-we-move-from-longhand-to-a-screen

Dredge, Stuart. "Spotify CEO Talks Covid-19, Artist Incomes and Podcasting (interview)." *Music Ally,* July 30, 2020. https://musically.com/2020/07/30
/spotify-ceo-talks-covid-19-artist-incomes-and-podcasting-interview

Dutens, Ludovic. "Leibniz to Christian Goldbach." Translated by Lloyd Strickland. *Opera Omnia,* April 17, 1712. http://www.leibniz-transla
tions.com/goldbach1712.htm

Dyer, Geoff. *But Beautiful: A Book about Jazz.* New York: Picador, 1996.

Dylan, Bob. "It's Alright, Ma (I'm Only Bleeding)." Recorded January 15, 1965. Track 10 on *Bringing It All Back Home,* Columbia Records.

Elgrably, Jordan. "James Baldwin, the Art of Fiction No. 78." *Paris Review,* issue 91 (Spring 1984). https://www.theparisreview.org/interviews
/2994/the-art-of-fiction-no-78-james-baldwin

Emerson, Ralph Waldo. "Experience." *Essays: Second Series.* Boston: James Monroe and Company, 1844.

Flake, Emily. "I Was in Charge of the Deck Chairs on the Titanic, and They Absolutely Did Need Rearranging." *McSweeney's Internet Tendency,* May 18, 2020. https://www.mcsweeneys.net/articles/i-was-in-charge-of-the
-deck-chairs-on-the-titanic-and-they-absolutely-did-need-rearranging

Frost, Robert. *Mountain Interval*. New York: Henry Holt, 1916.

Gaiman, Neil. "Neil Gaiman's 8 Rules of Writing." *Brain Pickings*, September 28, 2012. https://www.brainpickings.org/2012/09/28/neil -gaiman-8-rules-of-writing/

Hansen, Bert. "Hennig Brandt and the Discovery of Phosphorus." *Science History Institute*. July 30, 2019. https://www.sciencehistory.org/distilla tions/hennig-brandt-and-the-discovery-of-phosphorus

Harari, Yuval Noah. *Sapiens: A Brief History of Humankind*. New York: Harper Perennial, 2018.

Heffron, Jack. *The Writer's Idea Book 10th Anniversary Edition: How to Develop Great Ideas for Fiction, Nonfiction, Poetry, and Screenplays*. Cincinnati, OH: Writer's Digest Books, 2012.

Helman, Peter. "Max Martin Discusses Prince, Taylor Swift, and Pharrell in Rare Interview." *Stereogum*, February 27, 2017. https://www .stereogum.com/1926922/max-martin-discusses-prince-taylor -swift-and-pharrell-in-rare-interview/news

Hickey, Dave. *Air Guitar: Essays on Art & Democracy*. Los Angeles: Art Issues Press, 1997.

Hirway, Hrishikesh. "Episode 174: Meek Mill, 'Trauma.'" *Song Exploder*, December 11, 2019. https://songexploder.net/meek-mill

Hoagland, Tony, with Kay Cosgrove. *The Art of Voice: Poetic Principles and Practice*. New York: Norton, 2020.

Hyde, Lewis. *A Primer for Forgetting: Getting Past the Past*. New York: Farrar, Straus and Giroux, 2019.

Johnny Jet Editorial. "15 Tips for Surviving a Long Flight." *Johnny Jet*. December 22, 2018. https://www.johnnyjet.com/15-tips-surviving -long-flight-2

Kagge, Erling. *Silence in the Age of Noise*. Translated by Becky L. Crook. New York: Pantheon Books, 2017.

Kandinsky, Wassily. *Concerning the Spiritual in Art*. Translated by M. T. H. Sadler. New York: Dover, 1977.

Karr, Mary. *The Art of Memoir*. New York: HarperCollins, 2015.

Kaufman, Scott Barry, with Carolyn Gregoire. *Wired to Create*. New York: TarcherPerigee, 2015.

Kierkegaard, Søren. *Repetition and Philosophical Crumbs.* Translated by M. G. Piety. New York: Oxford University Press, 2009.

King Jr., Martin Luther. "I've Been to the Mountaintop." April 3, 1968, Memphis, TN. https://www.americanrhetoric.com/speeches/mlkive beentothemountaintop.htm

King, Stephen. *On Writing: A Memoir of the Craft.* New York: Scribner, 2000.

Klinkenborg, Verlyn. *Several Short Sentences About Writing.* New York: Vintage Books, 2013.

Konnikova, Maria. "How to Beat Writer's Block." *The New Yorker*, September 18, 2017. https://www.newyorker.com/science/maria-konnikova /how-to-beat-writers-block

Krakauer, Jon. *Into the Wild.* New York: Villard Books, 1997.

Kurutz, Steven. "David Bowie: Invisible New Yorker." *New York Times*, January 16, 2016. https://www.nytimes.com/2016/01/17/fashion /david-bowie-invisible-new-yorker.html

Lamott, Anne. *Bird by Bird: Some Instructions on Writing and Life.* New York: Anchor Books, 1995.

Lanier, Jaron. *Ten Arguments for Deleting Your Social Media Accounts Right Now.* New York: Henry Holt, 2019.

Lanier, Jaron. *Who Owns the Future?* New York: Simon & Schuster, 2013.

Leonard, Elmore. *10 Rules of Writing.* New York: William Morrow, 2007.

Levin, Janna. *Black Hole Blues and Other Songs from Outer Space.* New York: Knopf, 2017.

Light, Alan. *The Holy or the Broken: Leonard Cohen, Jeff Buckley, and the Unlikely Ascent of "Hallelujah."* New York: Atria, 2012.

Lorca, Federico García. "Theory and Play of the Duende." Translated by A. S. Kline (2007). Lecture, Buenos Aires, 1933. https://www.poetryin translation.com/klineaslorcaduende.php

Mandel, Leah. "Lucy Dacus on Being True to Yourself." *The Creative Independent*, June 6, 2019. https://thecreativeindependent.com/people /musician-lucy-dacus-on-being-true-to-yourself

Mann, Denise. "7 Tips for Getting Pregnant Faster." WebMD, archived. https:// www.webmd.com/baby/features/7-tips-getting-pregnant-faster#1

Manson, Mark. *The Subtle Art of Not Giving a F*ck: A Counterintuitive Approach to Living a Good Life.* New York: HarperOne, 2016.

Martin, Steve. *Born Standing Up: A Comic's Life.* New York: Scribner, 2008.

McPhee, John. *Draft No. 4: On the Writing Process.* New York: Farrar, Straus and Giroux, 2017.

Mitchell, Anaïs. *Working on a Song: The Lyrics of "Hadestown."* New York: Plume, 2020.

Monk, Thelonious. "T. Monk's Advice." Transcribed by Steve Lacy. 1960. https://www.openculture.com/2017/12/thelonious-monks-25 -tips-for-musicians-1960.html

Moorcock, Michael. "Michael Moorcock's Rules for Writers." *The Guardian.* February 22, 2010. https://www.theguardian.com/books/2010/feb /22/michael-moorcock-rules-for-writers

Mueller, Pam A., and Daniel M. Oppenheimer. "The Pen Is Mightier Than the Keyboard: Advantages of Longhand Over Laptop Note Taking." *Association for Psychological Science*, June, 2014. https://cpb-us-w2 .wpmucdn.com/sites.udel.edu/dist/6/132/files/2010/11/Psychologi cal-Science-2014-Mueller-0956797614524581-1u0h0yu.pdf

Murakami, Haruki. *What I Talk About When I Talk About Running.* New York: Knopf, 2007.

MusicTech. "How to Write Better Songs with Pro Advice from Jez Ashurst, Bernard Butler and More." September 3, 2019. https://www .musictech.net/guides/essential-guide/write-better-songs-advice-jez -ashurst-bernard-butler

Nelson, Maggie. *Bluets.* Seattle, WA: Wave Books, 2009.

Nemerov, Howard. "Speaking Silence." *The Georgia Review* 29, no. 4 (Winter 1975). https://thegeorgiareview.com/posts/speaking-silence

Nunez, Sigrid. *The Friend.* New York: Riverhead Books, 2018.

Odell, Jenny. *How to Do Nothing: Resisting the Attention Economy.* Brooklyn, NY: Melville House, 2019.

Oppezzo, Marily, and Daniel L. Schwartz. "Give Your Ideas Some Legs: The Positive Effect of Walking on Creative Thinking." *Journal of Experimental Psychology: Learning, Memory, and Cognition* 40, no. 4 (2014): 1142–52. https://pubmed.ncbi.nlm.nih.gov/24749966

Orwell, George. "Politics and the English Language." *Horizon* 13, no. 76 (1946): 252–65. https://www.orwellfoundation.com/the-orwell-foun dation/orwell/essays-and-other-works/politics-and-the-english -language

Pascal, Blaise. *Pensées*. Rev. ed. Translated by A. J. Krailsheimer. London: Penguin Classics, 1995. (Orig. pub. 1670.)

Passman, Donald. *All You Need to Know About the Music Business*. New York: Simon & Schuster, 2019.

Pattison, Pat. *Writing Better Lyrics*. Cincinnati, OH: Writer's Digest Books, 2009.

Pirsig, Robert M. *Zen and the Art of Motorcycle Maintenance: An Inquiry into Values*. New York: Harper Perennial, 1974.

Popova, Maria. "James Baldwin's Advice on Writing." *Brain Pickings*, February 8, 2016. https://www.brainpickings.org/2016/02/08/james -baldwin-advice-on-writing

Pressfield, Steven. *The War of Art: Break Through the Creative Blocks & Win Your Inner Creative Battles*. New York: Black Irish Entertainment, 2002.

Questlove, with Ben Greenman. *Creative Quest*. New York: Ecco, 2019.

Reuters Staff. "Fact Check: In the Event of a Fire, Yale Library Reduces Oxygen Levels in Book Stacks Only." *Reuters*, February 15, 2021. https:// www.reuters.com/article/uk-factcheck-yale-library-fire/fact-check-in -the-event-of-a-fire-yale-library-reduces-oxygen-levels-in-book -stacks-only-idUSKBN2AF1FN

Robinson, Matthew. "Myspace Apologizes after Losing 12 Years' Worth of Music." *CNN*, March 18, 2019. https://www.cnn.com/2019/03/18/us /myspace-lost-12-years-music-uploads-apology-intl-scli/index.html

Ross, Valerie. "5 Obscure Formulas that Rule the World." *Discover*, July 12, 2012. https://www.discovermagazine.com/the-sciences /5-obscure-formulas-that-rule-the-world

Ruefle, Mary. *Madness, Rack, and Honey: Collected Lectures*. Seattle, WA: Wave Books, 2012.

Sacks, Oliver. *Musicophilia: Tales of Music and the Brain*. New York: Vintage Books, 2007.

Sagan, Carl. *Contact*. New York: Simon & Schuster, 1985.

Saltz, Jerry. *How to Be an Artist*. New York: Riverhead Books, 2020.

Saunders, George. *The Braindead Megaphone*. New York: Riverhead Books, 2007.

The Search for Signs of Intelligent Life in the Universe. Directed by John Bailey. Los Angeles: Orion Classics, 1991.

Segall, Laurie. "Steve Jobs' Last Gift." *CNN Business*, September 10, 2013. https://money.cnn.com/2013/09/10/technology/steve-jobs-gift/index.html

Shaw, George Bernard. *Man and Superman*. Westminster: Archibald Constable & Co., Ltd, 1903.

The Simple, Sweet Life. "10 Things I Wish I Knew About Cookie Decorating." January 13, 2019. https://thesimple-sweetlife.com/things-i-wish-id-known-cookies

Smith, Patti. *Just Kids*. New York: Ecco, 2010.

Smith, Zadie. "Rules for Writers." *The Guardian*. February 22, 2010. https://www.theguardian.com/books/2010/feb/22/zadie-smith-rules-for-writers

Smith, Zadie. *Swing Time*. New York: Penguin Books, 2016.

Solnit, Rebecca. *A Field Guide to Getting Lost*. New York: Penguin Books, 2005.

Solnit, Rebecca. "How to Be a Writer: 10 Tips from Rebecca Solnit." *LitHub*, September 13, 2016. https://lithub.com/how-to-be-a-writer-10-tips-from-rebecca-solnit

Solnit, Rebecca. *Wanderlust: A History of Walking*. New York: Penguin Books, 2000.

Sondheim, Stephen. *Finishing the Hat: Collected Lyrics (1954–1981) with Attendant Comments, Principles, Heresies, Grudges, Whines and Anecdotes*. New York: Knopf, 2010.

Sontag, Susan. *Against Interpretation, and Other Essays*. New York: Farrar, Straus and Giroux, 1966.

Spiegel, Amy Rose. "Ocean Vuong on Being Generous in Your Work." *The Creative Independent*, May 16, 2017. https://thecreativeindependent.com/people/ocean-vuong-on-being-generous-in-your-work

Star Wars Episode V: The Empire Strikes Back. Directed by Irvin Kershner. Beverly Hills, CA: 20th Century Fox, 1980.

Storr, Will. *The Science of Storytelling*. London: William Collins, 2019.

Strayed, Cheryl. *Wild: From Lost to Found on the Pacific Crest Trail*. New York: Knopf, 2012.

Thompson, Derek. *Hit Makers: How to Succeed in an Age of Distraction*. New York: Penguin Books, 2018.

Thoreau, Henry David. "Walking." *The Atlantic*, June 1862. https://www .theatlantic.com/magazine/archive/1862/06/walking/304674

Time. "Books: You Too Can Write." (Review: Edmund Bergler, *The Writer and Psychoanalysis*.) March 6, 1950. http://content.time.com/time/sub scriber/article/0,33009,858702,00.html

The Times. "Jhumpa Lahiri Q&A: The Author of *Interpreter of Maladies* Answers Your Questions." September 8, 2004. https://www.thetimes .co.uk/article/jhumpa-lahiri-qanda-kb2zc6kmk53

Tweedy, Jeff. *How to Write One Song*. New York: Dutton, 2020.

Tweedy, Jeff. *Let's Go (So We Can Get Back): A Memoir of Recording and Discording with Wilco, Etc.* New York: Dutton, 2018.

Vuong, Ocean. *Night Sky with Exit Wounds*. Port Townsend, WA: Copper Canyon Press, 2016.

Vuong, Ocean. *On Earth We're Briefly Gorgeous*. New York: Penguin Books, 2019.

Watts, Alan. *The Wisdom of Insecurity: A Message for an Age of Anxiety*. New York: Vintage Books, 1951.

Zeigarnik, Bluma. "On Finished and Unfinished Tasks." *Psychological Research* 9 (1927): 1–85.

Zollo, Paul. *Songwriters on Songwriting*. Cambridge, MA: Da Capo Press, 1991.

INDEX